Monday Morning
Motivation

Also by David Cottrell

Monday Morning Choices

Monday Morning Mentoring

Monday Morning Leadership

Monday Morning Customer Service

Monday Morning Communications

136 Effective Presentation Tips

175 Ways to Get More Done in Less Time

Birdies, Pars, and Bogeys: Leadership Lessons from the Links

Becoming the Obvious Choice

David Cottrell's Collection of Favorite Quotations

Escape from Management Land: A Journey Every Team
    Wants Their Leader to Take

Listen Up, Customer Service

Listen Up, Leader

Listen Up, Teacher

Leadership . . . Biblically Speaking

Leadership Courage

Management Insights

The Leadership Secrets of Santa Claus

The Manager's Coaching Handbook

The Manager's Communication Handbook

The Manager's Conflict Resolution Handbook

The Nature of Excellence

The Next Level: Leading Beyond the Status Quo

Winners Always Quit! Seven Pretty Good Habits You Can
    Swap for Really Great Results

www.cornerstoneleadership.com

THE ONLY FORMULA YOU NEED TO
GENERATE POSITIVE ENERGY AT WORK

Monday Morning
Motivation

Five Steps to Energize
Your Team, Customers,
and Profits

David Cottrell

HARPER
BUSINESS

An Imprint of HarperCollins*Publishers*

HarperCollins books may be purchased for educational, business, or sales promotional use. For information, please write: Special Markets Department, HarperCollins Publishers, 10 East 53rd Street, New York, NY 10022.

This book is a revised and expanded edition of *Leadership Energy*, which was published by CornerStone Leadership in 2008.

FIRST EDITION

Library of Congress Cataloging-in-Publication Data
Cottrell, David,
    Monday morning motivation : five steps to energize your team, customers, and profits / David Cottrell.
        p. cm.
    ISBN 978-0-06-185938-0
    1. Employee motivation. 2. Leadership. 3. Organizational behavior.
4. Success in business. I. Title.
    HF5549.5.M63.C689   2009
    658.3'14—dc22   2009018886

09   10   11   12   13   OV/RRD   10   9   8   7   6   5   4   3   2   1

To every courageous leader who has been blessed with the privilege of motivating and energizing his or her team to become the best.

And to Albert Einstein . . . who probably never conceived that his theory of relativity would be the basis for successful leadership in the twenty-first century. Cheers!

Contents

Part Three
Optimizing Your Resources

Preface

Only a life lived for others is a life worthwhile.
—ALBERT EINSTEIN

November 10, 1980, was just another day . . . until I received a call.

On the other end of the phone was my manager, Fred Collins, who shared the news: "Xerox is reorganizing, and some new opportunities are coming up. Can you meet me in Memphis as soon as possible?"

The next day, I was offered a sales manager position. At twenty-six years old, I became one of the youngest sales managers at Xerox. From that day forward, my role changed from individual contributor to leader. I was confident and full of vim and vigor, ready to help our sales team become the best.

I quickly realized that my perspectives about work were different than most of my colleagues. Everyone did things differently—not necessarily bad, just different. It became an obsession of mine to mold a group of fourteen strong-willed sales reps into a team focused on team goals as well as their individual goals.

What I discovered—and then rediscovered throughout my career—was that, by and large, people want to be successful and do a good job. Of course, there are some exceptions who are only interested in their personal agendas, but most people want to be productive, achieve results, and work for a winning organization.

I also discovered that one of the key reasons many people fail or give up is because they lose their motivation and energy, often because the organization itself lacks motivation and energy.

While working at FedEx, I was responsible for twelve districts, each run autonomously. Those districts were provided with identical training and the same corporate resources. There were some geographical differences, but overall the districts were more similar than dissimilar. However, their results ranged from outstanding to mediocre. My "aha" moment came when I discovered that the difference in performance was a direct correlation of how the local management teams generated energy. Some of the local managers behaved in ways that generated negative energy, while others generated positive energy.

That experience stuck with me, and over the years I noticed that the way leaders manage their personal energy and the energy of their teams can mean the difference between success and failure. While reading about Albert Einstein one day, it occurred to me that his famous equation $E=mc^2$ was a powerful analogy for leadership energy. The Leadership Energy formula—and this book—were born.

Monday Morning Motivation is the third in our *Monday Morning* trilogy. *Monday Morning Mentoring* focuses on leadership development, while *Monday Morning Choices* is a guide to personal development. *Monday Morning Motivation* will help you create an organization full of energy and vitality. It is an accumulation of almost thirty years of trials, errors, failures, successes, and observations. I've studied people and what contributes to effective behavior in organizations, and I know the principles outlined in the book work!

Monday Morning Motivation is filled with lessons that will energize your team, your customers, and your profits. Enjoy!

David Cottrell
Horseshoe Bay, Texas

Part One

The Power of Energy and Motivation

Introduction

Not everything that counts can be counted,
and not everything that can be counted counts.
—SIGN HANGING IN ALBERT EINSTEIN'S
OFFICE AT PRINCETON UNIVERSITY

Albert Einstein's formula $E=mc^2$ has been called the most celebrated equation of all time. Breathtaking in its simplicity yet revolutionary in its impact, his formula fundamentally transformed scientific thinking about the universe.

Einstein's equation, which directly evolved from his work on the theory of special relativity, challenged well-established theories about mass and energy. Up until 1905, when Einstein developed his theory, scientists believed that mass and energy were two different things. Einstein was the first to propose the radical idea that mass and energy are two forms of the *same* thing and that neither appears without the other.

Einstein's theory was so revolutionary at the time that there was no way to verify it—and in fact, another twenty-five years would pass before anyone *could* prove it. Years later, his deceptively simple formula laid the groundwork for the development of both nuclear energy and nuclear weapons. In many ways, Einstein's theory changed the course of human history. Talk about a formula that's had a powerful impact!

Einstein's groundbreaking equation even reaches beyond the realm of science. By borrowing some of his principles and applying them to the world of business, we can explain the energy that is found in successful, high-achieving organizations. Like Einstein's formula, the Leadership Energy Equation, $E=mc^2$, is based on simple principles. But don't let its simplicity fool you. In combination with the accompanying straightforward techniques, the Leadership Energy Equation has the power to transform your organization.

First, though, let's address the question that's probably on your mind: What is organizational energy?

In trying to define organizational energy, perhaps it's useful to first define what it's *not*. Organizational energy is *not* short-term enthusiasm for the latest corporate program-of-the-month, and it is *not* a week-long buzz that follows the annual conference or executive weekend retreat. Although emotions like excitement and enthusiasm are often a byproduct, organizational energy itself is grounded in something much deeper—a solid commitment to an organization, its mission, and its values.

Organizational energy is also inextricably linked to individual motivation. At first glance, it might appear that energy and motivation are essentially the same thing, but they are, in fact, quite distinct. Energy gives you the physical ability to do something, whereas motivation gives you the emotional desire. Anyone who has ever suffered from chronic fatigue or has dealt with the effects of chemotherapy will tell you that you can be motivated all day long, but without energy, there is no action. You might desperately want to go play golf, spend time with the kids, or return that client call, but you simply don't have the energy to make it happen. On the other hand, as long as you have energy, you will find something to be motivated about and take action on.

"Motivation needs energy before it can empower you to achieve your targets," says personal empowerment consultant Aislinn O'Connor. Likewise, sports psychologists tell us that positive energy enhances motivation and fuels peak performance. In business, positive energy strengthens and solidifies personal motivation, producing an unshakable desire within each individual to achieve bigger and better results.

The potential for this positive energy, and the resulting motivation, resides in every employee, every team, and every department within an organization. But tapping into and releasing that energy is a task for an organization's leaders. And once the energy has been released, leaders must then find a way to focus that energy to achieve the organization's goals.

Admittedly, organizational energy is one of those concepts that's difficult to define and measure. But as Einstein so brilliantly realized, not everything that counts can be counted. There's no denying that organizational energy is a powerful force that fuels the success of many high-achieving organizations.

Monday Morning Motivation is a blueprint showing how successful organizations and their leaders use energy to drive individual motivation in order to survive and thrive in any economic condition. In fact, creating a vital and energetic team will allow you to leapfrog over your competition during even the toughest economic times. The techniques offered in this book will provide you with the necessary tools to harness the energy of your organization, move it to higher levels of achievement, and emerge from any economic condition stronger and more resilient.

The $E=mc^2$ equation is the only formula you need to generate positive energy and motivation at work. And the best part? You don't have to be an Einstein to learn and apply its principles. All you have to do is be willing to invest about one hour each week for ten weeks. That's it. No big new program or complex process. Just ten hours over two-and-a-half months. Here's how you do it:

- Find at least five other leaders (the more the better) in your organization who will join you for Motivation Mondays. Look for colleagues who are committed to the organization and who are willing to pay a small price to help their team achieve better results.

  Why Monday and not some other day? Because Monday is without question the most important day for organizational energy and personal motivation.

Monday sets the tone for the entire week. When people dread Mondays, the energy of the entire organization is sapped. But when Mondays are greeted with anticipation, the organization is energized and tends to stay energized all week long.

Monday is the key to your workweek. What if your Motivation Mondays created just 10 percent more positive energy and motivation for your organization? That could mean the difference between barely surviving and prospering!

- Make sure everyone has a *Monday Morning Motivation* book. During the week, each of you should read the chapter that will be discussed the following Monday (this will take thirty minutes or less).

- Arrive at work thirty minutes early for the next ten Mondays prepared to discuss the questions at the end of each chapter you've read.

- Make a commitment to take action on the concepts the group discusses and write your action items in the space provided at the end of each chapter.

- Notice how your team's energy and motivation stay revved up throughout the week.

Of course, you could do this by yourself, but I strongly recommend you invite others to join you. It's easier to make changes when you have supportive people around you to encourage you, act as a sounding board, and push you to move forward.

Just as important, when multiple leaders simultaneously generate more positive energy within their teams and focus that energy, momentum will be created within the organization as a whole. Over time, that momentum will generate enough positive energy and motivation that your team and your profits will take off like a rocket.

The single greatest influence on your organization's energy is the leader . . . you are the ultimate energizer. The energy you create can be positive or negative, and that energy is multiplied in the organization because of your impact on every member of your team. If you follow the steps outlined in this book, you will create and multiply positive energy that will lead to lower turnover, greater productivity, and higher profits. As a result, *you* will experience less stress, better results, and greater job satisfaction.

Read, enjoy, and apply *our* revolutionary leadership formula $E=mc^2$.

The Formula: E=mc²

Let's begin with a more detailed look at Einstein's famous formula **E=mc²** and an assessment of each element.

In this equation, known as Einstein's theory of special relativity:

E represents **energy**;
m represents **mass**;
c^2 represents **the square of the speed of light in a vacuum**.

In its simplest nonmathematical form, Einstein's equation states that energy and mass are equivalent and interchangeable—two different forms of the same thing.

When you think about this amazing concept you start

to appreciate Einstein's genius. According to Einstein, every
object—a book, a lawn chair, a can of tuna—is really a reservoir of energy just waiting to be unlocked. But we can unlock
the energy of mass *only* by multiplying it by the square of the
speed of light. Given that the speed of light is such an enormous number (670 million mph) and its square is even more
enormous, you start to realize that you don't need much mass
to produce a very large amount of energy. In fact, if we could
completely convert the very small mass of a paperclip (0.03
oz) into pure energy using Einstein's formula, we'd have the
energy equivalent of 18 kilotons of TNT—roughly the size of
the bomb that destroyed Hiroshima!

Now let's look at the leadership version of

$$E=mc^2$$

E represents your organization's **energy**;
m represents **mass**—the people within your organization;
c represents the **conductors that transmit energy**;
and ^{2} represents **your leadership energy** and **the multiplier effect it has on your organization**.

Recall in Einstein's theory how c^2 is the secret to unlocking
energy from mass? It's no different in this equation, in which
c^2 represents the power of your leadership. Your organization
already contains an awesome amount of energy, but only the
force of your leadership can release it and multiply it throughout your organization. In fact, the mathematical notation c^2

aptly illustrates the *exponential effect* that a leader can have on multiplying the energy that exists within an organization.

The Conductors of Leadership Energy

After the leader has released the awesome energy of an organization, is the leader's task complete?

No, the leader must then take a very important second step: to conduct that energy and focus it appropriately throughout the organization. Motivation within organizations is dependent upon positive energy being released and negative energy being minimized or even eliminated.

You're probably already familiar with the concept of an energy conductor—a medium that transmits energy, either along it or through it. To use an everyday example, your cookware is an energy conductor that allows you to focus heat energy to accomplish your goal: cooking dinner.

Leadership energy must be conducted too, so that it can be focused to accomplish the organization's goals. There are five key energy conductors available to us as leaders:

- **Synchronization.** With this conductor the leader can ensure that all the parts of the organization are working together toward a common goal.

- **Speed.** Leaders can resolve conflicts quickly and bring swift, decisive action if adjustments are required in the organization's strategic focus or management procedures.

- **Communication.** With this conductor the leader can connect the team members to corporate goals and ensure everyone understands their roles in accomplishing the mission.

- **Customer Passion.** Leaders focus the organization on the connection with its customers and creating customer loyalty, which in turn will provide the profits necessary for continued growth.

- **Integrity.** With this conductor the leader can ensure the organization adheres to fundamental values like honesty and truth in everything it does. Unlike the other conductors, however, integrity is more like a master switch for the organization. If integrity is compromised the other conductors are unnecessary since the organization's energy will be entirely depleted and the organization itself may be irreparably harmed.

Organizational energy is fluid and the energy conductors must be managed and balanced continuously. When any of the conductors are missing in an organization, negative energy will creep in and eventually dominate the positive energy that exists.

Let's use an example to demonstrate how all these concepts work together in an organization.

A team leader leaves an organization, but the team members continue to bring energy to all their tasks. After a while, though, and despite their best efforts, the team members find that without a leader their work lacks direction and purpose, and one by one they lose their energy, motivation, and vitality. Before you know it, productivity lags, sales goals are missed, and the once-energetic team members lose their effectiveness. There is no motivation or energy remaining that will help the team move forward.

Now assume instead that after a short period this team gains a new leader who is committed to the goals and ideals of the organization. Before long, the efforts of the team gain momentum and direction. As the leader grows in her role, she ensures the team is synchronized and working toward the same goals, she encourages communication throughout her organization, and she models integrity in all her relationships. In response the team members are continually reenergized, and they achieve even more. This leader has very effectively released the energy of her team, conducted it through the right channels, and focused it on achieving goals. Together, this team will have a powerful impact and will achieve their goals!

Positive vs. Negative Energy

Organizational energy can be either positive or negative. Positive energy, which promotes passion, satisfaction, and other affirmative emotions among team members, is possible when the team is focused on shared activities that support the organization's goals. Teams with consistent positive energy achieve greater results, experience less turnover, and have a higher level of job satisfaction.

Negative energy, on the other hand, results in tension and fear among team members, who often feel threatened. But if there is a high level of negative energy, it does not necessarily have to be a destructive force. In fact, this negative type of atmosphere is sometimes a good short-term motivator for intensely competitive team members who thrive on a seek-and-destroy mentality and can unite with other members against a common "enemy." But for long-term sustained success, extreme negative energy will divide team members, create job dissatisfaction, inhibit results, and ultimately create turnover. Negative energy works against the organization.

Signs of Positive Energy	Signs of Negative Energy
Deadlines are met	Deadlines are ignored
Sales and production goals are achieved	Sales targets and production goals fall short
Customer service is prompt and pleasant	Customer service is lacking
People recognize and acknowledge one another	People complain and nitpick
People are problem solvers	People are problem makers
Excellence is the norm	Mediocrity is acceptable

Maintaining Your Personal Leadership Energy

We all have times when our leadership energy level is not as high as we'd like it to be. Workplace conflicts, tight deadlines, customer demands, employee performance issues—all of these are common situations that can easily sap a leader's energy. And since you have the most influence over your team's energy level, if you lose your energy, the entire team will lose its energy as well.

So what can you do to refuel when your leadership energy level is low?

1. **Get back to the basics.** What are you trying to accomplish? What are your goals? What is your purpose in the organization? Clarifying your personal mission will create energy for you.
2. **Get more involved with your team.** Involvement, collaboration, and teamwork generate positive energy.
3. **Give energy away.** Act enthusiastically even if you don't feel enthusiastic. The energy you give away will be abundantly replenished. Energy (positive and negative) is contagious! If you are enthusiastic, others around you will become enthusiastic. Their enthusiasm, in turn, will cause you to be more genuinely enthusiastic.

The Formula Summary

$E = mc^2$

E represents **energy**

m represents **your people**

c represents the **conductors of energy**:

- Synchronization
- Speed
- Communication
- Customer Passion
- Integrity

^{2} represents the **leader's impact** on the organization

Monday Morning Discussion Questions

- What is your personal energy level—low, high, or somewhere in between? Is your energy mostly positive or negative?

- What is the energy level of your team and of the organization as a whole? Is your team's energy mostly positive or negative? How about the organization's energy?

- What specifically can you do to refuel the next time your leadership energy level runs low?

Three Things You Will Do This Week to Generate Positive Energy

1. _____
2. _____
3. _____

Why Energy and Motivation Leaks Occur

The only source of knowledge is experience.
—ALBERT EINSTEIN

Remember your first helium-filled balloon? Remember the special feeling of walking along with the balloon tied to your wrist, letting it float above your head? When you took it home you let it float to the ceiling of your bedroom. No matter how many times you pulled it down that first day, the balloon was so filled with helium it always floated back up to the ceiling.

But the next morning, you awoke to find a sad blob of latex on the floor. What had happened to that cool balloon that was floating on the ceiling when you went to bed? From the outside, nothing appeared to have changed—there were no holes, and the ribbon was still tied tightly around the end. But even so, the helium had leaked out, and the once-mighty balloon had lost its ability to stay aloft.

The same thing happens to some organizations. For a while the organization is filled with so much energy, enthusiasm, and motivation that it seems to soar, and the sky's the limit. But then, slowly, the energy eventually leaks out, and the organization becomes a mere shadow of its former self. Perhaps from the outside nothing obvious has happened, but somehow the energy that sustained it has disappeared, sometimes seemingly overnight. What was once a super-energized, highly motivated group now struggles to achieve the organization's goals.

How does it happen? Energy leaks from the organization just as helium or air leaks from a balloon. When this happens, quick action will be needed to stop the leak and replenish or replace the energy. In Part Two, we'll discuss the energy conductors that leaders can use to refuel and recharge their teams when energy leaks occur. Now let's look at the three most common causes of energy and motivation leaks within an organization: burnout, comfort in the status quo, and decay.

The Burnout Leak

If an organization is constantly pushed beyond its limits by leaders trying to drive it to spectacular short-term results, it will eventually burn out and begin leaking energy. If every month is a "crisis," soon the organizational norm is the crisis mode. Not many people can function effectively in the crisis mode all the time. They will eventually burn out.

Organizational burnout can be caused by a supercharged market or aggressive growth strategies that can stretch employees too thin. It may occur because of an overzealous production schedule, overtime hours, lost weekends, or lack of a break between new product rollouts.

Do you remember the heady days of the 1990s when the dot.com boom was followed by the dot.com bust? As the dot.com bubble kept growing, leaders earned enormous bonuses, software developers gained VIP status, and sales records soared into the stratosphere—and what could be better? Unfortunately for some organizations, energy began seeping out because continued overexertion made it difficult to think about anything other than maintaining the drumbeat that gradually became louder and louder, faster and faster. The energy was being burned out of organizations of all sizes. For many, the focus was on the right now with little time and energy devoted to the long-term results. There were few strategies being implemented that would help them sustain energy and keep energy in reserve to survive not only tomorrow but also the next day and the next day after that.

Fortunately, many organizations did have energy in reserve after the dot.com bust, and as a result were agile enough to move into the next generation of business. Others, however, especially those unaware of their energy leaks, were unable to adjust and finally collapsed.

Organizational and leadership burnout can also occur in the opposite conditions—in tough economic times when companies are in financial distress or face sudden or drastic downsizing. The work still has to get done, but there are typically fewer people and resources available to do it. Organizations in this type of crisis mode can get by for a time, but eventually something has to give.

To stop the burnout leakage of energy, it's important to understand that organizations and individuals function best when there's a rhythm—intense energy surges followed by less intense phases. No one can maintain the highest level of intensity for an extended period of time. That would be like driving your car at maximum speed all the time. Eventually, you'd blow out your engine. Your organization, just like your automobile, requires consistent maintenance, refueling, and tune-ups.

BURNOUT SYMPTOMS

Is your team leaking energy due to burnout?

Place a check next to any symptoms your team is experiencing:

__ Constantly operating in survival mode

__ Increase in number of sick days

__ Prolonged increase in overtime

__ Reductions in productivity

__ Things often fall through the cracks

__ Exhaustion and stress

__ Interpersonal conflicts and short tempers

__ Little or no time for development

__ Poor communication

__ Ends justify the means

__ Extended or superfast growth

__ Short-term focus

The Status Quo Leak

After a long period of success in a fairly stable environment, sometimes the energy of an organization leaks out because the organization grows too comfortable with the status quo. People are lulled into doing things the way they've always done them and resist making the changes that are needed to restore energy and improve performance.

Or sometimes status quo energy leaks occur after a long period of lackluster performance, during which the organization has lost confidence. In either case, the result is that the organization is weak and lifeless, and often it becomes unable to recharge and leverage its resources.

With a status quo energy leak, employees have a relatively high satisfaction level without having high emotions. In fact, low-intensity emotions are usually the hallmark of companies satisfied with the status quo.

Because everyone is satisfied—in their jobs and by their performance—these companies are marked by weak vitality, low levels of alertness, and insufficient stamina to make changes. If the words "But we've always been successful doing it this way" are familiar, it's time to check your organization's energy level to ensure you're not being lulled into inertia by the status quo.

The status quo leak is difficult to address because things seem to be okay the way they are. After all, maintaining market share, profits, and acceptable turnover numbers is doing better than some. Why change?

Complacency—being satisfied with the status quo—is the

root of mediocrity. High performers are rarely satisfied with the status quo and continually search for the next level of performance. Unfortunately in many organizations those high performers are punished for their high-energy and personal drive. The result is that the very best people will leave the organization or eventually conform to the status quo. That is not a good deal for the high performer or the organization.

If you look at the organizations that have failed in your community over the past twenty years, in many cases the energy leaked due to their focus on maintaining the status quo as opposed to staying in front of the pack. The successful organizations are the ones that were not content with the status quo and were able to maintain the energy necessary to sustain success.

To prevent the status quo leak, you must have a feedback system in place with your team, your customers, and other external sources. If asked for their opinion, they will provide you with the information you need to progressively move forward. Internal feedback alone has the potential to contribute to the status quo energy leak.

STATUS QUO SYMPTOMS

Is your team leaking energy because it has become too comfortable with the status quo? Place a check next to any symptoms your team is experiencing:

___ No forward movement toward organizational objectives

___ Lack of innovation, creativity, and fresh ideas
___ Paralysis of analysis
___ High resistance to change
___ Dispassionate, unmotivated team members
___ Deteriorating profitability
___ High performers leaving or underperforming
___ Lack of drive to stay ahead of the competition
___ No clear direction or defined goals
___ "Way we've always done things" mentality
___ Little value placed on customer feedback

The Decay Leak

The third type of energy leak happens because of decay in an organization, which may be the worst and most toxic leak of all. Many times, these decay energy leaks are solely the result of internal issues. The small, insignificant internal leaks are subtle but over time will drain energy from an organization. Some of the most common are:

- time and energy wasted in unproductive and ineffective meetings;

- lack of clarity in communication resulting in inefficient processes and procedures;

- paralysis of forward movement because of the fear of making difficult decisions;

- lack of a positive organizational culture;

- power struggles while jockeying for power and position;

- and nourishing a victim mentality by allowing blaming and complaining.

Although seemingly small, the cumulative energy lost through these leaks could easily make the difference between surviving and prospering.

Another type of decay leak typically occurs when an organization is struggling with major internal *and* external problems such as a lack of vision, labor contracts that prevent agility, losing touch with customers, and not keeping up with market trends. The energy the organization once used to compete must be diverted to address these challenges.

General Motors is an example of an organization that's been hit hard by a combination of internal and external issues. Battered by a triple whammy—the financial problems of its GMAC Finance subsidiary, labor issues with the United Auto Workers union, and stiff foreign competition—it's no surprise that GM lost its energy.

Once the giant stabilization of American industry, GM is now losing money, creating huge layoffs, and accepting bail-out money from the U.S. government to survive. The bail-out money may address its short-term needs, but for long-term survival, GM will have to address the decay that has been building up for years. Its competition has changed the playing field even though GM was one of the founders of the industry. GM has allowed decay to exist for so long that the company's leaders are convinced the system is the problem, refusing to acknowledge the internal and external decay.

DECAY SYMPTOMS

Is your team leaking energy because it's experiencing decay? Place a check next to any symptoms your team is experiencing:

___ Major external challenges such as regulatory changes, the economy, etc.

___ Labor problems

___ Absence of strategies to stay abreast of market trends and conditions

___ Organizational confusion; lack of clarity

___ Negative organizational culture

___ Customer service problems or loss of customers

___ Discontentment; lack of harmony and unity among team members

___ Increases in turnover

___ Apathy

___ Office politics

___ Poor communication

The Road to Recovery

Once massive amounts of energy leak from an organization, is survival possible? Absolutely. But it requires the effective use of the five energy conductors—synchronization, speed, communication, customer passion, and integrity. Let's take a look at Motorola for inspiration.

Motorola—once the world leader in communications technology—came to be known as the Bleeding Giant in the early years of this century. In its seventy-five-year history, the company that invented the cell phone and a number of other major innovations had lost its mojo. Its technology was outdated, and it lagged far behind competitors. Product quality, which had slipped abysmally in only a few years, was at its lowest point. Quarter after quarter, Motorola continued to miss financial targets, hemorrhaging profits and people (hence the nickname the Bleeding Giant). Leadership seemed puzzled about where to go and what to do next.

The company's vibrant energy all but gone, Motorola was now scrambling to keep up while its more aggressive competitors raced ahead with new and exciting technology. A new CEO was named as restructuring and downsizing were under way. Sixty thousand of its 150,000 worldwide workforce were laid off.

Once the CEO and his new leadership team were on board and able to assess the communication giant's problems, 34 percent of management—men and women who didn't want to take responsibility for quality and customer satisfaction—were replaced with leaders who shared Motorola's core values and had courage and a sense of urgency. Management's key job was identified as more than just overseeing day-to-day operations. Added to that was keeping track of industry trends and figuring out what they meant for Motorola. This added responsibility was required because the communications industry was not only consolidating but also converging with the computing and entertainment industries.

The now-transformed leadership team used energy conductors to stop the bleeding. First, they generated positive energy by creating a shared vision, passion, and commitment. Next, they formulated a plan to make sure that everything they did was in alignment with their corporate objectives. This step included spinning off the corporation's semiconductor unit so Motorola could focus on its core strengths.

They also ensured their reward system was in sync with their goals. With quality as the focus, Motorola began giving bonuses to workers for increased quality and customer satisfaction, first for a 10 percent improvement and then for a 20 percent one. Meetings were focused on quality improvement and assessing competing products, something that had been previously ignored.

One of the Bleeding Giant's biggest challenges had been speed—the ability to outpace competitors by delivering innovative products at a rapid rate. Motorola needed to go from 30 mph to 70 mph. The new CEO worked to inspire people to win by coaching the management team and helping them hire good people. In return, he expected flexibility, agility, and the ability to think quickly and move rapidly on every decision.

Next, they developed a communication process to ensure

that all employees knew how they fit into the goals of recovery. Town hall meetings were held, employee surveys were distributed, and input and innovation were solicited. Motorola's values were marketed to the employees, establishing the importance of every job at every level. Said one manager, "We marketed to 60,000 employees every day—and they got it!"

Motorola also listened to its customers. It recaptured its customers' trust with an innovative lineup of new products, including the red-hot Razr line. This boosted Motorola's market share of the handset business from 13 to 19 percent, moving its financials back into black ink. Soon after this successful launch, the newly emerging communications leader also developed the first iTunes compatible cell phone—the Rokr. With renewed strength and synergy, dollars were redirected into new technology research and development, and Motorola began building toward wire line, wireless, and cable conversion—something leadership called "seamless mobility."

Under new leadership and new strategies around synchronization, speed, communication, and customer passion, Motorola immediately began turning around. Clearly, revitalizing corporate energy is not easy. Far from it. The task of replenishing an organization's energy is not for the faint of heart. It requires a dedicated leadership team to understand why the leaks occurred and to develop a plan to revitalize the energy within the organization.

Energy Leaks Summary

If energy is leaking from your organization, the first step must be to identify the cause. If you determine it's a huge leak, perhaps it was caused by a sudden or dramatic event that was uncontrollable. Or it may have been the result of more subtle events—burnout, the comfort of the status quo, or decay. Perhaps the loss has resulted from the cumulative effect of smaller energy leaks over time. Regardless of how the leak began, it has to be addressed immediately.

Second, learn from the energy loss and regroup. It is probably not too late to recover but it will take courage and immediate action to stop the leak and generate positive energy. In most cases, the best choices for re-creating organizational energy start from within with an inspiring new vision, a simplified mission, or new organizational values. We'll take a quick look at some of those in the next chapter.

Energy Leaks

- Burnout—constant intense energy over an extended period of time

- Status quo—long periods of consistent performance without new challenges

- Decay—leaks that result from failure to address external or internal issues

Monday Morning Discussion Questions

- Is your team experiencing large energy leaks due to burnout, status quo, or decay?

- Can you identify any small energy leaks that have a big impact on your team, such as inefficient meetings or processes, poor communication, office politics, etc.?

- What situations or events cause your personal energy to leak?

Three Things You Will Do This Week to Stop Energy Leaks

1. —————————————————————————
2. —————————————————————————
3. —————————————————————————

Mass: Building the Right Organization

Measured objectively, what a man can wrest from Truth
by passionate striving is utterly infinitesimal.
—ALBERT EINSTEIN

M*erriam-Webster Unabridged Dictionary* defines mass as "an aggregate of particles or things making one body." And that is precisely how we will define the mass in our Leadership Energy Equation. Mass is the aggregate of employees that make up the organization. Therefore, every organization has mass, and this mass is critical to the organization's growth and continuance.

The people on your team—the mass—possess tremendous potential to achieve your goals and ensure your success. However, you must first ensure you have an organization capable of producing positive energy by putting the right people in the right places.

Identifying Energizers and Sappers

In theory, every person on your team is a source of energy for your organization. But in reality, some team members create energy while others sap or destroy energy. If you know your team well, you already know which team members are sappers and which ones are the energizers.

High-energy performers test the limits and spur themselves and others on to even greater results. These are the people who will push you up and add energy to your reservoir. They spark others to perform. It's fun to watch them in action. A team full of energized people is typically easy to motivate but challenging to manage because their high energy level requires constant direction and focus.

At the other end of the spectrum are the sappers. You know who they are—they complain and whine, and think of every reason possible why plans and strategies will not work. They are the people who pull you down and sap your energy. They blame others for their issues and don't accept responsibility for what they control. Their negativity and cynicism effectively sucks the energy right out of the room. A team dominated by energy sappers is relatively easy to lead because there is little forward movement or activity. But it is very challenging to motivate these team members to achieve results because they are content with mediocrity.

Energizers	Sappers
High-performing superstars	Low-performing falling stars
Accountable	Don't accept responsibility for their actions
Enthusiastic with a positive attitude	Cynical and tend to complain and nitpick
Driven	Complacent
Focus on high-priority objectives	Easily distracted by time wasters and mindless tasks
High productivity seems effortless (they typically operate "in the zone")	Productivity drags (almost as if they're tied to an anchor)
Stress is low	Stress is high

Your organizational energy is not the sum of your individuals. It is dependent upon the ratio of energizers to sappers. If you have more sappers than energizers, the energy will be drained, and in fact the energizers may eventually become sappers. As unfortunate as it is, a negative, cynical person has a far greater impact on the energy of the team than a positive person. He or she will deplete far more energy than a positive person will add. That is not fair, but it is reality. Adding a positive energizer does not counter a sapper; in fact it probably takes at least three energizers to counter the energy drained by one sapper.

Many people think having a sapper on the team is better than having no team member at all. If the sapper works in isolation, that may be true. However, since most employees are part of a team or a department, a sapper is usually worse than not having anyone at all. The reason: One sapper on a team of energizers is like having one dead battery with three energized batteries in the remote control. Eventually the dead battery, or the sapper, will drain the energy from the others. As a leader you must prevent the sappers from destroying the energizers.

Critical Mass

"Critical mass" is a term with both scientific and social foundations. In the scientific realm, it means the number or amount large enough to produce a specific action or desired result. It takes a certain amount of material—the critical mass—to initiate a nuclear reaction. Less material . . . no reaction.

In social terms, critical mass represents the point at which there exists enough momentum in a movement for the movement to sustain itself and even expand on its own. For example: "The national uproar over drug abuse has reached critical mass in Washington."

In business, we can define critical mass as the point at which enough employees act in such a way as to cause a shift in the entire organization. It is also the point at which the desired shift becomes a movement capable of sustaining and growing itself. Culture change is a prime example. You won't see a shift in the organization's culture until enough individuals change their attitude, thinking, and behavior.

With respect to organizational energy, the goal is to achieve critical mass—the point at which enough individuals are maximizing their energy that the energy of the entire organization is increased.

How many employees does it take to achieve critical mass?

Two? Twenty? Two hundred? Two thousand? The answer depends on many factors—the size of the organization, the current culture, the leadership's effectiveness, and the level of trust that exists between leadership and employees, just to name a few. And let's face it—you're never going to get *every* employee to do what needs to be done.

However, if you want to create change in an organization, you have to get to critical mass. You will achieve critical mass when momentum overtakes inertia. You will achieve an increase in organizational energy, for instance, when the forward momentum of the energizers in your organization exceeds the negative effects (or the inertia) of the energy sappers.

How do you achieve critical mass? It can be created by a large, sweeping factor such as a sudden shift in market conditions or the development of a revolutionary product. Such events tend to galvanize enough employees to create a permanent change. However, in most organizations, critical mass can be reached through:

1. establishing **dedication** to the organization's mission;
2. building a **commitment** to shared values;
3. and creating **leadership** critical mass.

Dedication to the Mission

The first critical step in aligning the organization is ensuring that everyone is on board with the organization's mission. Ideally that means every employee should buy into the leadership's vision of where the organization is headed. Buy-in happens when your team understands, commits, and takes action to support your organization's goals.

The key to having your team dedicated to the mission is simplification. Simplify everything so that everyone understands exactly what you are trying to accomplish. If your mission and purpose have not been clearly established, expect trouble ahead. A clearly defined, easily understood purpose is like the hub of a wheel—everything else is dependent upon the hub holding all the spokes together.

A large oil exploration company that wanted to improve its safety record tried several approaches, to no avail. Finally, the safety department figured out that its safety program would be successful only if it were able to gain the buy-in of every employee—regardless of title and responsibilities.

As with most new initiatives, the new safety program really couldn't be just a program. It had to become a way of life throughout the corporation. Management had to convince every employee it was in his or her best interest to participate.

How did they do it?

When the new approach to safety was presented, a small group of believers immediately saw the wisdom of trying to do things differently—but in a safer manner. Those people were the catalyst for others to also open their minds to new and different ideas.

Next, the organization's leadership began sharing stories that projected a positive future for the organization—what was in it for the workers if they embraced the new, different, but safer way of doing things.

Their safety mission evolved to "We go home every night in good shape."

The mission was simple and when the workers saw how it would impact their future, those employees sitting on the fence slowly but surely joined the early believers. In the next twelve months, the organization's safety record improved almost 50 percent. In addition, both employee satisfaction and customer satisfaction improved, creating more profit for the organization.

Without achieving critical mass (e.g., getting the buy-in of the company's workers at every level), the new safety culture would not have been realized.

People support what they help create. The more you involve your team in any cultural change, the greater your team will become dedicated to the mission.

Commitment to Shared Values

Shared values build trust and link every level of the organization together. They support the identity and mission, providing guiding principles that everyone on your team can aspire to practice. When people work for an organization with values that match their own, they feel a sense of satisfaction, rapport, and community.

You'll often find an organization's values posted in its reception area, on its Web site, or inside the front cover of its annual report. But values must be more than just a lofty statement that never makes it off the wall or the printed page—they must be at the core of the organization, and each member of the organization must make a concerted effort to uphold them.

Thomas J. Watson Jr., the son of the founder of IBM, understood that you need unyielding corporate values in order to be successful. He said, "I firmly believe that any organization, in order to survive and achieve success, must have a sound set of beliefs on which it premises all its policies and actions. Next, I believe that the most important single factor in corporate success is faithful adherence to those beliefs. And, finally, I believe if an organization is to meet the challenge of a changing world, it must be prepared to change everything about itself—except those beliefs—as it moves through corporate life."

The purpose of your organization is defined by the values promoted and communicated throughout the organization.

Almost every organization has published values. Even Enron, one of the most corrupt companies in recent history, had published values. Plaques stating its corporate values of respect, integrity, communication, and excellence covered the walls of Enron. Sounds sort of silly now, doesn't it? Values written on ink and paper are worthless unless the values become the driving force of the organization.

Whatever values you have chosen for yourself or your organization, they should be your constant barometer to measure your results. Anything that contradicts your stated organizational values must be eliminated.

When Michelangelo was asked how he carved the splendid statue of David out of a massive block of marble, he replied: "Simple. I just cut away everything that wasn't David." Your role is to cut away anything or anyone who contradicts the values of your organization.

Leadership Critical Mass

The final critical element to achieving critical mass within the organization's employees is to create *leadership* critical mass. Leaders throughout the organization must be in sync with one another. You can't hope to reach employee critical mass if your leadership team isn't together.

As with employees, the bulk of leadership should be dedicated to the organization's mission and committed to its values. And yet, that alone is not enough to generate leadership critical mass. Leaders throughout the organization should buy into and support all organizational initiatives. The best leaders are also the best followers.

The amazing power of leadership critical mass was evident in the rise of Barack Obama. Prior to 2007, Barack Obama was a relatively unknown senator from Illinois. Even in the early stages of his presidential campaign, he was considered too inexperienced by just about everyone except those within his own organization. Hillary Clinton had a double-digit lead for the Democratic nomination in every poll. Yet just one year later, Barack Obama was sworn in as the president of the United States. He not only defeated the Democratic front-runner, but also a far more seasoned and experienced Republican nominee.

This come-from-behind victory was the result of the depth and strength of Obama's organization. One of the foundations of his campaign strategy was to create a critical mass of leaders across the nation at the grassroots level. Candidate Obama believed that he could win the election by involving the mass of people who had never been involved in a presidential election before and their forward movement would energize the entire Democratic Party. He developed leadership not only in the key swing states, but also in the smaller states that the other candidates ignored or had written off. That critical mass of leaders and involved campaigners was then able to create and energize a critical mass of millions upon millions of voters . . . and the rest is history.

Leadership critical mass within organizations is developed by aligning leaders both vertically and horizontally. It's not enough for senior leadership to champion a cause, nor is it enough for front line supervisors to be on board. Leadership critical mass requires alignment at every vertical level of the organization—from the C-suite to senior leadership to middle managers to front line supervisors. Consider the effect on a team if their leader speaks negatively about her boss's decision to change a particular process or policy. Will the members of that team be energized about and supportive of the change? Not likely, because they see leadership chaos above them. On the other hand, when employees see that everyone in their line of leadership is on the same page, they are motivated to get on board also.

Keep in mind that alignment and agreement are not the same thing. Honest, constructive disagreement and people challenging the status quo are signs of a healthy organization. It also indicates that people are engaged and that their opinions and input are valued by the organization. But when leaders overtly disagree with a decision by upper management, even after their input has been genuinely heard and evaluated, team energy can quickly move in a direction away from where you were trying to go.

Leaders should also be aligned horizontally in the organization. Leadership critical mass involves alignment among leaders in every functional area of the organization rather than just a few departments such as marketing and sales. If leaders of various departments are not in sync, organizations experience the "silo effect," where each team operates almost independently of the others. This can lead to turf wars, finger pointing, and drops in productivity. As a result, energy is sucked right out of the organization.

When leaders in every department throughout the organization are in sync with one another and with the corporate mission, they are all on the same page, so to speak, working toward the same goals. This leadership critical mass leads to organizational critical mass as leaders ensure their individual team members are also aligned with the organizational goals and objectives. Bottom line: You can't create employee critical mass without first having leadership critical mass.

The Multiplier Effect

Once you have achieved both leadership and employee critical mass, dramatic shifts and redirections of the organization can be created by the smallest of changes, even in the largest companies.

To illustrate how a small change can have a huge impact, let's take a look at the "butterfly effect"—a discovery made by meteorologist Edward Lorenz. Lorenz used computer simulation to track and model weather patterns. He entered data on wind speed, air pressure, and temperature into three linked equations. The calculations formed a mathematical loop—the results of the first equation were fed into the second, the results of which were fed into the third equation. The output of the third equation was ultimately the input back into the first equation. By using the mathematical loop calculations, Lorenz found he could predict weather with some accuracy.

Most mathematicians check and recheck their calculations, and Lorenz was no exception. One day while rechecking the results of his complex weather calculations, Lorenz took a shortcut: he entered the same data he'd used previously, except he rounded each number to the nearest one-thousandth rather than to the nearest one-millionth. (For example, 0.506 instead of 0.506127.)

You'd think that this minor adjustment in the data would have only a minor impact on the overall results, perhaps no more than one-tenth of one percent, right? Yet when Lorenz examined the results, he was amazed to discover a significant difference in the two calculations. The infinitesimal change he made in the input was magnified by the feedback process in the mathematical loop, and the results were greatly altered. This discovery ultimately led the meteorologist to wonder, "Does the flap of a butterfly's wings in Brazil cause a tornado in Texas?"

Since then, the butterfly effect has become a familiar illustration to describe how a small change in a dynamic system can cause a chain of events that leads to large-scale change.

What does this have to do with organizational energy?

When you achieve critical mass—when the effect of your energizers is greater than the effect of your energy sappers—then small changes in leadership can have a significant impact on the organization. This is the multiplier effect of leadership.

Let's suppose your leadership team has communicated a crystal clear vision of its organizational goals. In addition, every person on the team understands his or her role and is committed to the mission. Without any other leadership activity, the team will perform at a standard baseline level. But with critical mass, when appropriate leadership energy is applied through the five energy conductors, the effect will be powerfully amplified.

On the other hand, if there is leadership chaos—when leadership is constantly changing directions, the reward system is out of sync with what is expected, or leaders are not in alignment throughout the organization—that confusion will also be magnified throughout the organization. Leadership chaos drains organizational energy. Leadership focus and direction add energy to the organization.

Each movement within the masses has a multiplier effect. With critical mass, even small leadership changes—positive or negative—have a tremendous impact. For instance, a seemingly small change of creating a crystal clear vision for your organization can influence both your team and your customers. People become energized when they have a mission . . . customers become energized when they are working with an energized team. Once you have your critical mass moving in the right direction, unbelievable results can occur. Our job as leaders is to increase the positive energy and move the masses to create the greatest and most positive impact, and to avoid leadership chaos that would have a negative impact.

Measuring Mass and Its Value

Most people will agree that human capital is a key to organizational success. But despite this fact, few organizations develop a comprehensive approach to maximize this resource and release all the energy of the organization.

Companies generally determine the value of the mass by measuring the number of employees, productivity per full-time equivalent, gross profitability, and the cost of those employees. Without question, all of these indicators are important. But the real value of the mass is found in the energy it can produce. Perhaps we should ask questions such as:

- How can we increase the energy within our workforce?

- What are we doing to drain energy from our team?

- How can we allocate our resources to gain energy?

Although mass has the capacity to generate energy for the organization, it is leadership that either blocks that energy or enables it to flow freely. To truly leverage the value of the mass, leadership must focus organizational energy through the use of the leadership conductors. They are the key to creating and sustaining organizational energy and moving the organization forward. Leadership conductors, therefore, are the focus of Part Two.

Leadership Actions That Create Energy	Leadership Actions That Block Energy
Clear, consistent vision	Constantly changing direction
Solicit input	Decisions without input
Rewards aligned with mission	Rewards not aligned with mission
Foster collaboration	Foster internal strife
Encourage positive change	Encourage complacency
Promote positive growth	Discourage new ideas
Meetings that are brief and to the point	Meetings that drag on

Mass Summary

The mass of your organization—its employees—have the potential to make or break your business. As a leader, one of your most important tasks is to build an organization with the right people. You'll then need to identify which team members create positive energy and which drain it so that you can sustain the team's energy level.

Your goal as a leader is to create critical mass within the organization—the point at which enough individuals are maximizing their energy so that the energy of the entire organization is increased. To do that, it's crucial that you create a team atmosphere that's aligned with the organization's goals. Energy will be created and sustained only when your team is dedicated to the organization's mission—leadership's vision of where the organization is headed—and committed to the organization's values. You must also achieve leadership critical mass, where leaders at all vertical levels and within all departments of the organization are in sync and aligned.

When you have leadership and employee critical mass, then you can take advantage of the multiplier effect, in which a small positive change in leadership creates a powerful impact throughout the organization. And finally, the value of the mass is not simply the employees themselves, but also their potential to produce organizational energy. Leadership's job is to clear the fog, create a route so that the team can see where they are going, and leverage the team's strengths through the energy conductors.

Mass: Building the Right Organization

- Team energy is dependent upon the ratio of energizers to sappers.

- A shift in organizational culture occurs when you achieve critical mass—when enough individuals change their attitude, thinking, and behavior.

- The best leaders are also the best followers.

- Organizational energy increases when the forward momentum of energizers exceeds the negative effects of the energy sappers.

- People support what they help create.

- Leadership focus and direction create energy. Leadership chaos drains organizational energy.

Monday Morning Discussion Questions

- What is the ratio of energizers to sappers on your team, and what effect does that have on the overall energy of the team?

- Does every employee on your team understand and support the organization's mission and goals?

- With respect to your team, are your organization's values actually practiced or merely posted?

- Are *you* dedicated to and supportive of the organization's mission, values, and initiatives? What can you do to further demonstrate your commitment?

- Are there situations within the organization where leaders are not in sync or aligned?

- As a leader, what do you do or say that might block your team's energy? What do you do or say that enables the team's energy to flow freely?

Three Things You Will Do This Week to Focus Your Team's Energy

1. _____

2. _____

3. _____

Part Two

The Conductors of Energy and Motivation

Synchronization
Speed
Communication
Customer Passion
Integrity

4

Synchronization

Any intelligent fool can make things bigger, more complex,
and more violent. It takes a touch of genius—and a lot of
courage—to move in the opposite direction.

— ALBERT EINSTEIN

Synchronized swimming, an Olympic sport since 1984, has always fascinated me. The only way to describe it is to call it upside-down ballet. It's beautiful to watch but also very demanding for swimmers, requiring fitness, stamina, and flexibility.

Synchronized swimming usually involves a team of swimmers who perform in perfect synchronization to music. The only equipment utilized by a synchronized swimmer is a nose clip.

As I've watched synchronized swim competitions, I've wondered how a team can stay perfectly in sync, especially when the team is performing upside-down and underwater—neither of which is natural for most human beings. Yet Olympic-caliber synchronized swim teams work in unison to create a breathtaking performance.

On world-class synchronized swim teams, each member must clearly understand every nuance of the choreography. All members must also know their individual roles, when to perform each move, and how each of them personally contributes to and affects the entire team's performance.

When every swimmer is in sync, the performance can be spectacular. But if even one team member were ever out of sync, chaos would result.

The same thing happens in business. Synchronization is absolutely fundamental to your organization. When all elements of your organization are in sync, its performance can be energizing, spectacular, and profitable. But without synchronization—if even one aspect of the organization is out of sync—people lose focus and stagnate. Before you know it, forward movement comes to a halt. The result can be chaotic—and often unprofitable too!

Two elements will help you attain synchronization within your organization: simplifying your objectives and aligning your reward system.

Simplify Your Objectives

Everything should be made as simple as possible, but not simpler.
—ALBERT EINSTEIN

If your people are out of sync with your organization's objectives, perhaps it's because they're confused about what those objectives are. Maybe your objectives are too complex, too illogical, or too difficult to comprehend and embrace. People are energized and more productive when they have memorable priorities to pursue.

Or perhaps your people are confused by the dizzying array of organizational objectives. Ever hear of "corporate attention deficit disorder"? Here's how it happens: One month, management's focus is to increase revenue. The next month, the focus is on decreasing costs. Then the hiring function is the priority, and thirty days later management is focused again on cutting back. Which one do your people choose to be in sync with?

What would happen if the synchronized swim team's choreography was too complicated? Or what would happen if the choreography changed that often? What would result—chaos or synchronization?

If your goals are constantly changing, you can count on constant chaos. Some in your organization will ignore the current goal because experience has taught them that the goal will soon change anyway. Why bother changing course now when another change is probably just around the corner?

You may be thinking that changing direction is not necessarily a bad thing. And of course you're right. Changing direction isn't a bad thing—as long as a crystal clear mission has been established, and as long as everyone understands that the changes will help them accomplish this mission. If that's true of your organization, change won't lead to chaos; instead, it can lead to success. However, everything must be in sync *before* the change.

Synchronization can effectively conduct energy *only* if everyone clearly understands what you're trying to accomplish. Simplicity is the key. Every employee should be able to clearly explain the direction the organization is taking and what role they have in achieving success.

O'Reilly Auto Parts is a successful fifty-year-old company in the intensely competitive auto parts industry. It has over 3,200 stores and is in thirty-eight states. Some industry insiders say that auto parts is a commodity business with little or no control over customers or success. O'Reilly thinks differently. They believe the future is determined by having every O'Reilly employee in sync with each store's objectives and with the corporate objectives.

O'Reilly has simplified its objectives by establishing a simple, three-pronged mission. The company aims to have the best-trained employees in the industry who deliver service over and above the customer's expectations and who overachieve their productivity targets.

When you walk into an O'Reilly Auto Parts store, you'll immediately feel the impact of that mission. You'll be greeted by a knowledgeable, well-trained associate who understands his mission: take care of the customer. In the home office, upper management clearly understands its mission: support the store personnel and help them achieve the store goals.

O'Reilly's list of priorities has only three words: people, service, productivity. Every O'Reilly employee knows the corporate mission and can recite it by heart in well under thirty seconds. If it takes you more time than that to recite your mission, it's probably too complex. Keep it simple.

If you can't explain it simply, you do not understand it well enough.

—ALBERT EINSTEIN

Thomas J. Watson Sr., the founder of IBM, was a master at taking a complex task and simplifying it so that everyone in the organization could understand and implement the objectives. He crafted IBM's famous (and ubiquitous) motto from a single word: "THINK." The motto epitomized Watson's devout rationalism. "All the problems of the world," he told his employees, "could be solved easily if men were only willing to think."

Watson was a man of action and it probably didn't occur to him that thinkers, having thought, sometimes failed to recognize that there is a time to quit thinking and take action. Since Watson's time, the global economy has undergone a tectonic shift, and the leaders at IBM have realized that the old motto was a little out of sync and changed its official slogan to "THINK. THEN DO." Still simple, easily understood, and implementable.

Align Your Reward System

Sometimes the reward system of the organization is out of sync with the organization's objectives. In fact, your reward system may be rewarding actions that are diametrically opposed to what you want to accomplish.

For example, in some organizations, employees are paid for overtime—which effectively says the slower you produce, the more money you make—but the organization is penalized for missing deadlines. Watch what you're rewarding and make sure it's in sync with your objectives.

Several years ago, Levi Strauss created an aspirations statement of company values to clearly define what the organization wanted to be. Among the values were teamwork, diversity, recognition, integrity, communication, and empowerment. Levi's values were certainly not unique; you'll find them on the walls of many organizations.

However, until a few years ago, Levi's employees were rewarded based only on how well they fulfilled their personal job descriptions. Many times, the job descriptions were out of sync with the aspirations statement. Understandably confused, employees' job performance suffered.

After a concerted effort, Levi Strauss achieved synchronicity by aligning its business objectives with its corporate aspirations. Every job description, performance review, and recognition program was aligned with the corporate aspirations. This leadership adjustment ultimately successfully reenergized the company to record profits.

Bottom line: Ensure that your reward system actually encourages employees to achieve your stated goals and objectives. That seems so obvious, and yet it's a mistake many organizations unwittingly make.

A major organization headquartered in the Midwest was growing rapidly based on its ability to fill same-day orders by 5:00 P.M. every day. A larger facility was in the works but wouldn't be ready for months. As growth continued, the orders were being filled later and later, and instead of being shipped at 5:00 P.M., they were going out the door at 6:00 or 7:00 P.M.

Faced with costly service failures and overtime, upper management followed an employee's suggestion and started paying all employees working in the fulfillment department until 7:00 P.M., whether or not it took that long to get all the orders out. Employees could go home when all the orders were out the door.

Suddenly, but not surprisingly, the day's shipments were processed and out the door by 5:00 P.M. Under the old system, employees were actually being rewarded for staying late by being paid overtime. When the reward system changed so that the reward was the possibility of leaving early, the results changed.

The old management axiom "What gets rewarded gets done" was proven once again!

Synchronizing When Things Are Out of Sync

A couple of years ago, Pitney Bowes was exploring strategic alternatives for Pitney Bowes Management Services (PBMS)—their outsourcing subsidiary responsible for client mail and document management solutions. PBMS employs over 12,000 in 1,600 client locations.

Several alternatives were being considered for PBMS, including the possible sale of its U.S. business. As is often the case, rumors were rampant in employee break rooms and questions arose at client sites. In the interim, work flow was strained as employees began to speculate about possible changes and the impact of these changes on employees and clients.

PBMS president Vince De Palma could see the negative impact the speculation was creating. Without taking swift and aggressive action, the business and its clients would suffer. That is when he and his management team came up with a plan to move PBMS employees and clients back in sync with the corporate Pitney Bowes objectives and refocus their business.

In order to work, the plan had to acknowledge the facts of their situation and the leadership team had to address the issues head-on. The leaders of PBMS devised a three-pronged attack to align their team back in sync to take care of business.

First, De Palma and his team created a new, clear, consistent, and simple direction that everyone could understand, follow, and implement. They had spirited, no-holds-barred debate to revise the business strategy, vision, and mission, which had transformed into more words than actions over the years. They then delivered the new strategy to employees and clients.

Next, they took actions to rebuild confidence through honest and open communications. Their employees and clients needed ongoing and consistent reinforcement that things were going to be okay. Every other week PBMS's top 300 managers participated in a conference call to hear strategies for the new direction. Led by the highest levels within the organization, the calls were unfiltered and unbiased. The first half of the call was about the direction; the second half was spent responding to questions about where the company was headed and why.

After the call, each of the managers was armed with specific talking points that they were to communicate with every customer within forty-eight hours. In addition, the managers had daily huddles with their direct reports to ensure everyone was in sync.

The third strategy was to increase upper management's visibility throughout the organization. It was critical that field personnel trusted the executive team and knew that upper management really cared. To address this, De Palma and his team created and distributed a quarterly video that addressed upfront the issues at hand. In addition, the senior executives would personally explain how the division was doing, what the year's results looked like, where the division was headed, and what everyone could do to improve results. They also increased the number of town hall meetings—two-hour sessions with the front line management—because they understood that the most thorough communication strategy is no substitute for face-to-face dialogue.

The results of the strategy?

What began as a time of uncertainty evolved to become a very energetic, creative, and successful period in the history of PBMS. The company gained clients. Turnover decreased. Employee engagement scores rose and EBIT grew.

De Palma's theme—action, authority, accountability, and agility—became more than just words on paper; it became a reality. Upper management, middle management, front line management, front line employees, and their clients were all in sync with PBMS's goals.

Was this an easy task? No way! All individuals have to do their part, pull their weight, and keep their eye on the mission. However, with team effort; clear, consistent, and sensitive communication; and a willingness to change long-standing paradigms, the winds of uncertainty disappeared and were replaced by a well-oiled, synchronized, and profitable division.

Synchronization Conductor Summary

Synchronization is fundamental to the efficient functioning of your organization. When all elements of your organization are in sync, you can more efficiently conduct energy throughout the organization for spectacular and profitable results. Without synchronization, however, people lose focus, stagnate, and paralyze the organization.

Synchronization can be created in two key ways: First, simplify your objectives so that everyone on the team understands what you're trying to accomplish. And second, align your rewards system with your objectives. When people are not accomplishing your organization's objectives, check out your reward system. You may find your employees are doing exactly what you're paying them to do.

The Synchronization Conductor

- Without synchronization, your organization will be paralyzed, and forward movement will come to a halt.

- Synchronization can effectively conduct energy only when everyone clearly understands what you're trying to accomplish.

- Confusion creates corporate attention deficit disorder. Clarity and simplicity lead to synchronization and the accomplishment of objectives.

- If it takes you more than thirty seconds to recite your corporate mission, it is probably too complex.

- What gets rewarded gets done.

Monday Morning Discussion Questions

- Is your team typically synchronized or chaotic? Why?

- Do all team members clearly understand the team's objectives and their role in achieving them? If not, who on your team needs more clarification?

- Is your reward system aligned with your objectives—are you rewarding the actions you want repeated? Are you rewarding any behaviors that are actually the opposite of what you want to accomplish?

Three Things You Will Do This Week to Enhance Your Team's Synchronization

1. _____
2. _____
3. _____

5

Speed

Imagination is everything. It is the preview of life's coming attractions.
—ALBERT EINSTEIN

Along Germany's famous high-speed autobahn freeway system, many accidents are caused by people who are driving too slowly. If you don't keep up with the pace, you get run off the road. The same theory applies in business, where reacting too slowly will leave you behind the competition or out of the race altogether.

The autobahn was designed to allow for fast travel between Germany's major metropolitan areas. Many people mistakenly think it is a single stretch of high-speed highway when, in fact, it is a sprawling infrastructure of roads built with features to accommodate speed and minimize accidents. Likewise, high-performing organizations have well-developed infrastructures that allow for greater organizational speed while also lowering the risk of "accidents" or strategic mistakes. This type of infrastructure enhances an organization's ability to be agile and to capitalize on new information quickly.

Organizational speed in its most basic form means decisiveness—understanding your goals, priorities, and customers so well that you can make crucial decisions quickly. Many organizations leak energy because their decision-making process is slow and weak. It's not clear who needs to weigh in on decisions or who has the final authority to make them. Interestingly, decision making can also be challenging in organizations where there's a lot of positive team energy—where everyone wants to contribute to every conversation and every decision. Inertia sets in as decisions are rethought and redebated. In both instances, speed is needed.

Speed also means agility and simplicity. To conduct energy throughout your organization, you need to react quickly and decisively in three key areas: in organizational strategies, in your management approach, and in conflict resolution.

Using Speed to Adjust Organizational Strategies

Every successful organization has to be agile and react swiftly to maintain its customers. If your organization can't react to the competitive market quickly enough, your customers will leave you behind.

Wal-Mart is one organization that has demonstrated its agility and the ability to change strategies rapidly. It's become the largest retail company in the world through its ability to quickly capitalize on the newest technology to manage inventory, distribute products, and handle cash. Wal-Mart uses technology to track customer buying trends and make quick decisions about which inventory needs to be available in each store. Sam Walton learned early on that speed could be the primary differentiator that would allow his organization to deliver the lowest prices to its customers.

When Sam Walton created Wal-Mart, his rules for conducting business were well ahead of his time. In fact, the principles he used to lead his company are still ahead of most organizations today. His focus on speed and using speed to help create loyal customers is an integral part of Wal-Mart's success.

For instance, when a hurricane is headed toward a coastline, Wal-Mart buyers begin preparing for the event long before it hits. In addition to procuring the typical hardware items, Wal-Mart buyers know exactly which food items people in the hurricane's path will need and stock their stores days in advance. (By the way, in case you're wondering, the number one food item sold is Pop-Tarts . . . strawberry flavor.) It's Wal-Mart's carefully constructed infrastructure that allows it to react with such speed and flexibility.

Case in point: Wal-Mart has a catastrophe plan already in place to help local communities when unexpected disasters hit. In 2007, a "rain bomb" hit Marble Falls, Texas. Marble Falls is a town of about 10,000 people in the Texas Hill Country. The rain bomb dropped nineteen inches of rain in six hours—now you know why they call it a rain bomb. The water supply in

Marble Falls was cut off and electricity was out for over a week. Residents were stranded without electricity or fresh water even though they had just received nineteen inches of rain.

Within twelve hours of the rain bomb, Wal-Mart had trailer trucks full of water available for the community—free to all. The local store manager, Daryl Holley, and many of his employees, along with other volunteers, distributed the water in the local Lowe's parking lot because Wal-Mart was too far outside of town for many residents to get to. For over a week, fresh water was available to every person who needed it courtesy of Wal-Mart.

There are plenty of people who criticize Wal-Mart for many things. However, the folks of Marble Falls, Texas, will never forget when Wal-Mart called upon its massive resources and utilized the speed conductor to connect with its customers and to provide help in a crisis situation.

Wal-Mart has used speed for new product introductions as well. In an effort to increase sales to its loyal customers who frequently spend time in the sporting goods department, Wal-Mart asked Hormel Foods to come up with a snack that could be sold on the fishing and hunting shelves. Within weeks, "Spamouflage"—Spam in camouflage cans—was being sold at Wal-Mart! The largest organization in the world has mastered the art of using speed to its advantage.

How does Wal-Mart do it?

Wal-Mart has identified speed as one of its strategic advantages. The company created an infrastructure that gives leaders throughout the organization—from the marketing department to store managers—the autonomy and the resources to act quickly. Wal-Mart has taken the concept of speed and drilled it all the way through the company so that the Daryl Holleys of the organization can make the necessary adjustments to better serve their customers. Its strength of reacting quickly and efficiently is one of the reasons why Wal-Mart seems to be able to maintain sales regardless of economic conditions. In fact, during the most uncertain economic times, Wal-Mart has managed to grow sales while almost every competitor's sales have been flat or down from previous years.

ReStrategize Me

A few years ago, filmmaker Morgan Spurlock produced a documentary called *Super Size Me* that skewered the fast food industry, and McDonald's in particular, by chronicling his monthlong experiment on the health effects of a fast food diet. For one month, Spurlock ate three meals a day at McDonald's. The results were frightening: his weight shot up more than a pound a day, and his triglycerides and cholesterol went through the roof. Twenty days into filming, his doctors begged him to stop.

The movie's release, just months after two teenage girls had sued McDonald's for causing their obesity (they lost), dealt a blow to the McDonald's brand. Without realizing it, McDonald's had been leaking energy for years. The company had become comfortable with the status quo, with the notion that it was the king of fast food. It ignored the marketplace and societal trends toward healthier eating and living.

To regain its energy in the marketplace and make up for lost market share, McDonald's made several significant, agile moves to adjust its corporate strategies: the company icon, Ronald McDonald, abandoned his clown costume and donned exercise clothing; heart-healthy items like salads and fresh fruit were added to the menu; CDs and exercise DVDs were offered with certain menu items; and nutritional information was printed on food wrappers.

Another significant move was the hiring of Mary Dillon, former president of Quaker Foods, as executive vice president, global chief marketing officer, and leader of McDonald's Balanced Lifestyle Initiatives. The company also began redesigning its restaurants to include such features as TVs, Wi-Fi connections, and separate areas for families. And in an effort to align with growing consumer interest in the quality, sourcing, and ethics of products, McDonald's recently switched its supplier of both coffee beans and milk.

What would have happened if McDonald's had sat back and waited for the storm of negative publicity or the "fad" of healthier lifestyles to pass? Would the company have been able to survive? We'll never know; but we do know that by moving quickly to make strategic adjustments, McDonald's regained its energy and entered into a new era of success.

Using Speed in Management Processes

Speed is particularly critical in two key areas of employee relations: recognizing employees who perform and dealing with employees who underperform.

Recognizing Employee Performance

Recognizing positive individual and team performance is an essential ingredient in creating and maintaining organizational energy. Front line employees stay with an organization for one key reason—because they feel that their supervisors care about them. When employees feel appreciated they perform better, and that translates to less attrition and happier customers.

And it doesn't take much to show you care. Even relatively simple gestures, like writing positive e-mails or promptly returning their calls, go a long way in creating an atmosphere of appreciation. The entire organization is energized by an environment where people are appreciated.

In 2007, the Beryl Companies, a leading U.S. health care customer service firm, was second on the Great Place to Work Institute's annual list of best medium-sized companies to work for in America. Why do people enjoy working at Beryl, and why is its turnover rate significantly below the industry average? Beryl does many things extremely well, but the driving force behind employee satisfaction is CEO Paul Spiegelman, who understands the power of positive recognition.

Spiegelman says the emotional environment is where culture is built. And so Beryl laid the foundation with a simple yet powerful personal recognition strategy that's based on sending personal note cards to coworkers every day, recognizing milestones such as anniversaries and birthdays, and helping those in need.

BerylCares is the name of the behind-the-scenes program that gathers information about events in a worker's life. Says Spiegelman, "We can't recognize births, weddings, and other

joyful happenings and then turn a blind eye to personal ca-
lamities. Instead, we reach out very quickly if someone is going
through a rough time due to a health situation, a death in the
family, or just a patch of rotten luck. If there's anything we can
do as a company to help and support them, we want to know
about it and acknowledge it. If our culture preaches taking
care of our own, the caring has to start in my office."

Acknowledging employees is vitally important to maintaining the organization's energy.

While I was at FedEx, we had a recognition program called
Bravo Zulu. In the U.S. Navy, the Bravo Zulu flag means "well
done." Every FedEx manager had Bravo Zulu stickers, plaques,
and money he or she could use to immediately recognize any
employee who went above and beyond in an effort to satisfy a
customer.

The Bravo Zulu symbol was prominently displayed at
every FedEx office. People wore the symbols on their employee
badges, put them on their business cards, and posted them at
their workstations. Bravo Zulu was a symbol of pride, and it
was effective because it was a quick, immediate reward. The
Bravo Zulu sticker cost a mere five cents, but the recognition
was priceless.

Both Beryl and FedEx understand that acting quickly to
recognize employees can have a tremendous impact in building loyalty, respect, and trust. Those qualities in turn build
positive energy for your organization.

Dealing with Underperformers

As much as you might want to avoid it, it's vital to take quick, decisive action to stop the energy leaks caused by underperformers. These are the people on your team who chronically do as little as they can get away with, or who are simply not right for the job.

Though usually small, this group can have a huge impact because they also prevent the top performers from doing their jobs. To compensate for these underperformers, you're probably loading up your top performers with extra work just so you can meet your deadlines. You don't mean to punish your star performers, but by asking them to take up the slack for nonperformers you're punishing them for doing a good job. So what's the incentive for a top performer to keep working at that level? Once they see that mediocrity gets rewarded, they may gravitate to mediocrity too—exactly the opposite of what you need.

---

7 WAYS TO ADDRESS MEDIOCRE PERFORMANCE

1. Hire people who have the talent, desire, and ability to do the job well.

2. Clearly communicate responsibilities and expectations. Confirm understanding.

3. Provide training and make continual learning a top priority.

4. Regularly provide specific performance feedback. Make sure people know how they're doing long before performance review time.

5. Consistently recognize and reward positive performance.

6. Hold people accountable for negative behavior and performance.

7. Set the example. Be a positive role model for the team.

What's worse, the problem of an incompetent employee will not just go away by itself. When people figure out they can do less and still get rewarded, they'll just continue to underperform if there's no reason to do more. And while you're giving them their second or third "one more chance," they could be destroying your team and your organization. The longer an underperformer remains on the team, the more positive energy will be sapped and the more negative energy will be created.

The leader's job is to reward superstar performance and create new positive energy, so you must deal with the falling stars quickly, decisively, and fairly.

You may be saying, "But it takes too long and it's too hard to get rid of the underperformers. It's easier just to move the work around." Yes, it's true that in many organizations it is difficult to fire anybody—and normally speed is not part of the firing process. But there's a huge price to pay when you allow people to stay around after they've already "quit."

The rules of employee termination are in place to make sure you're fair and consistent—not to prevent you from ridding your organization of someone who's chosen not to work to the performance standards. In fact, your human resources department will be a great help if you've done your job by establishing performance standards and providing feedback to your employees about their performance. If you want to fire someone to whom you gave a great performance review just two months ago, don't make the situation worse by blaming HR for making it too tough!

If the employee's performance doesn't improve after you've given feedback to that employee, then even Vince Lombardi wouldn't be able to turn "her" around. There are reasons for that person's poor performance, but you don't control those. What you do control is the next move in your organization—do you allow underperformers to stay and drain your team's energy, or should you allow them to move forward with another organization?

Most laid-off employees will eventually admit that getting fired was the best thing that ever happened. As unbelievable as that may sound, many people who have been fired are forced to move from a job that isn't right for them to something more aligned with their talents and interests. With few exceptions, it's also the best thing for the team and the leader.

Here's an exercise I did several years ago that opened my eyes to the courage it takes to manage varying performance levels:

First, on a flip chart, write the name of each team member and then categorize each one as either a superstar, middle star, or falling star.

Post each member's most recent performance review score next to his name. Next, retrieve his personnel file. For each person, make a notation beside his name on the flip chart showing each time that you've documented some kind of recognition or performance improvement over the past six months. It could be a letter of appreciation or a performance improvement document.

You may discover, as I did, that there was little difference between how I treated my top performers and the lowest performers. The issue in my case was not an employee issue—it was a leadership issue of not recognizing and rewarding the behaviors I wanted.

Here are seven questions to ask yourself, as the leader, to better understand why a team member might be underperforming:

1. Are my expectations crystal clear?
2. Are my expectations reasonable and fair?
3. Has each team member received adequate training to do the job properly?
4. Does each team member understand *why* it's important to do the job correctly?
5. Am I holding each team member accountable for his or her performance? Are there appropriate and consistent consequences for nonperformance?
6. Have I given each team member the freedom to be successful?
7. Have performance obstacles been removed?

If you can honestly answer yes to all seven of those questions, you have done your job. The issue lies with the employee.

Deal with any underperformers quickly yet fairly. The

longer an underperformer remains on the team, the more energy will be sapped from your team

Using Speed to Resolve Conflicts

We can't solve problems by using the same kind of thinking we used when we created them.

—ALBERT EINSTEIN

Various studies show that most adversity inside organizations involves interpersonal conflicts within the work group. Those same studies show that very few of these conflicts work themselves out without third-party intervention, and it is estimated that more than 50 percent of managers' time is spent dealing with conflicts. The cost of that time—not even considering lost sales and productivity—is enormous; many experts estimate the cost of conflict is well over a thousand dollars per incident!

You've probably experienced firsthand the realities and consequences of conflict in the workplace: the projects that are derailed; the energy that unresolved disagreements steal from you and your team; the negative impact on productivity; the missed targets, goals, and deadlines. Just one incident can be so stress-inducing and unpleasant that it wipes out the whole day, evening, and sometimes the entire week. One manager recently said, "When someone comes to me about a conflict, everything stops. I have to turn away from my work and help them. The time and energy it takes to step in and help them work something out is very draining. And the rest of the team is watching—they usually know about the conflict before it ever gets to me."

It's no wonder we see conflict as a huge pain in the neck!

But there is good news: conflict *can* lead to progress. Most of the inventions, discoveries, and technological advances made throughout history have been the result of humans developing solutions to conflicts. Disagreements among scientists, explorers, and philosophers lead us to learn more about our world and ourselves.

In business, conflict handled calmly, skillfully, and with speed is an opportunity to create positive change. It offsets inertia, acts as a catalyst for an organization, and stimulates creativity and problem solving. In fact, too little conflict—settling for the status quo—may be just as harmful as too much conflict.

The key to managing conflicts in the workplace is to address them quickly. As tempting as it may be, don't make the mistake of ignoring conflicts, hoping they'll just go away. The longer conflicts are allowed to fester, the more likely they are to drain energy from the work group and from the entire organization.

A popular rule of thumb in dealing with conflicts is called the 1–10–100 rule. Generally, the concept is that the longer conflicts exist without being addressed, the more expensive and time consuming they will be to fix. For example, if a conflict between two people is solved quickly and efficiently, it can be solved with the equivalent of one unit of time, money, or resources. That same problem—if it's not addressed and spreads throughout a work group—will require the equivalent of *ten* units of time, money, or resources to solve because more emotions and perceptions must be addressed. If the problem spreads throughout the organization or into the customer base, it will require at least *one hundred* units of time, money, or resources to solve. That is one hundred times what it would have cost to solve the same conflict in the beginning! In other words, what began as a molehill has now evolved into a mountain.

When conflicts are ignored, tremendous organizational energy is diverted from moving forward to dealing with the conflict. The rule illustrates how a small issue can grow exponentially if left unchecked. The longer it persists, the more difficult and time consuming it is to fix—and the more of your organization's energy it will waste.

You can apply the 1–10–100 rule to many situations in an organization—a minor conflict between two team members, a billing discrepancy with a customer, a slippage in quality, or a simple misunderstanding with a vendor.

The only exception to the rule of handling conflicts quickly is when you are personally involved. In those situations, the best strategy is to put some time between the other person's action or behavior and your reaction. Give yourself some time to clear your head, calm down, and think through the situation rationally.

A wise person once stated: "Never leave a nail sticking up where you find it." In other words, don't just ignore minor problems, hoping they'll go away. Put speed to work in your organization to resolve small conflicts quickly, before they become expensive, company-wide disasters!

WAYS TO PREVENT A CONFLICT FROM ESCALATING

1. Get all the facts and clearly identify the problem.

2. Encourage people to challenge the status quo often so that alternatives are continually being evaluated.

3. When others explain their intention and viewpoints, summarize and paraphrase to confirm understanding.

4. Look for common ground in any difficult situation.

5. When possible, resolve one issue at a time.

6. Deal with the molehills before they become mountains!

7. Only send and respond to e-mails that are informational in nature. If there is any hint of disagreement, meet in person or pick up the phone.

8. Watch and listen for inconsistencies between people's words and their nonverbal behaviors and encourage them to voice their concerns.

Speed Conductor Summary

With the pace of change these days, all businesses are in the business of speed. But the speed conductor isn't just about doing things fast. It's about agility and decisiveness.

If your organization has been left behind competitively, or if your strategies are outdated and no longer profitable, show agility and make the necessary changes.

In your management approach, celebrate successes by quickly recognizing high performers. Quick, on-the-spot action to recognize the achievements of employees can have a tremendous impact in building loyalty and respect. And although it's a painful task, take decisive action to clear out the underperformers from your organization. The longer they stay, the more energy they drain.

And finally, if there's a conflict in your organization, don't ignore it. Instead, recognize immediately that it probably won't be resolved without intervention and act decisively to resolve it before it grows out of control. Large problems consume far too much time, energy, and resources that are needed elsewhere in your organization.

The Speed Conductor

- To remain on top, successful organizations have to be agile and react swiftly to changing conditions.

- The entire organization is energized by an environment in which people are appreciated.

- Front line employees stay with an organization for one key reason—because they feel that their supervisors care about them.

- It is vital to take quick, decisive action to stop the energy leaks caused by underperformers.

- Acting quickly to recognize employees can have a tremendous impact on building loyalty, respect, and trust.

- The longer an underperformer remains on the team, the more energy will be sapped from your team!

- Problems do not just go away. Address issues quickly to avoid larger problems later.

Monday Morning Discussion Questions

- How often do you recognize positive individual and team performance?

- How do you treat your superstars as compared to your underperformers?

- Are there any consistent underperformers on your team? What are you doing to deal with them quickly, decisively, and fairly?

- Do you tend to ignore problems and conflicts, hoping they will go away, or intervene quickly to try to resolve them?

Three Things You Will Do This Week to Develop Your Agility and Decisiveness

1. _____

2. _____

3. _____

6

Communication

The important thing is not to stop questioning.
Curiosity has its own reason for existing.
— ALBERT EINSTEIN

Twenty area vice presidents sat around the conference table. The rules had been outlined. All VPs knew this was their chance to improve the operation of their organizations. After the facilitator had put everyone at ease, she fired the first question: "What one thing would make the greatest difference in your area?"

One by one, the VPs slid their written responses toward the facilitator. Without exception, every one of them had written "improved communications."

"You can't have too much in the way of communication," said one VP when the results were announced. "It's the foundation of your effectiveness."

According to a communications return on investment (ROI) study conducted by Watson Wyatt in 2006, that VP was right. The study found that companies with effective internal communications were 4.5 times more likely than other companies to report high levels of employee engagement. Employee engagement, in turn, had a positive impact on the bottom line:

- Companies with the most effective internal communication programs achieved a 91 percent total return to shareholders (TRS) versus a 58 percent TRS among ineffective communicators.

- Companies that significantly improved their internal communication effectiveness increased their market share by 19.4 percent.

Communication is an important energy conductor in any organization, continually carrying energy internally to all parts of the organization and externally to customers and vendors.

But how do you create this communication conductor? Build numerous small meeting rooms throughout corporate headquarters to encourage random conversations? Start a company newsletter? Make sure every employee gets a copy of the annual report? No. The most important element of the communication conductor is to connect the corporate goals and objectives with the activities of your team.

Some elements of effective communications can include the following:

- using technology to connect employees;

- creating a formal communication structure and process;

- facilitating a connection between employees and customers;

- dealing quickly and directly with issues;

- soliciting employee feedback;

- and integrating rewards in the organizational culture.

The communication conductor begins even before employees are hired, in the way they're treated in interviews. Communication conductors never end.

Communicating Appreciation to Employees

During a recent exit interview in a large New York City–based corporation, a high-level employee sat across from the organization's president and explained her reasons for leaving. "I've done more than the job required, I've been a loyal employee for almost eight years, and I've never had anything but superior performance reviews," she said. "Yet I have rarely felt appreciated or valued."

The president was dumbfounded. "But we've paid you very well for your efforts," he responded after a moment.

"But I need more than the money," the employee answered.

"Our benefits are some of the best in the industry."

"But I need more than benefits," the woman said. "I need to know that I'm worth the same care and concern I give every one of my customers—and to be honest, I've never sensed that from this organization." Even though the employee was well paid, good at her job, and valued by the company, she felt that the organization really didn't care about her. The organization's emphasis on pay and benefits was not as important to her as the very simple act of making sure she knew that someone cared about her.

In 1998, study results published in the *Harvard Business Review* noted that retailing giant Sears reported a 4 percent increase in employee satisfaction. This increase, in turn, resulted in an identical increase in customer satisfaction and a rise of more than $200 million in revenue. Coincidence? Not likely.

Southwest Airlines' mission statement says: "Above all, employees will be provided the same concern, respect, and caring attitude within the organization that they are expected to share externally with every Southwest customer." At Southwest, management expects employees to "give as good as they get"—and the yield is very high. Employees treat customers with care and compassion because that's what the organization

provides for them—and this corporate culture keeps customers coming back, year after year.

To conduct energy through your organization, you must
stay connected through good communication.

"As one example, at Southwest, leaders and managers are
taught in training classes to write commendation letters for
their employees," explained Lorraine Grubbs-West, author of
*Lessons in Loyalty: How Southwest Airlines Does It—an Insider's
View.* "Employees are encouraged to commend their fellow
workers—and Southwest tries to make it easier by providing
simple forms called stroke sheets."

Every time a stroke sheet is written, two things happen:
First, the person who wrote the letter receives a letter of thanks
from the company for commending a fellow employee. Second,
the employee being recognized receives a copy of the commendation plus a thank-you from the department head.

"At Southwest, we identified 'internal customers' as well
as 'external customers,' " Grubbs-West explained. "The pilots'
major internal customers, for example, were the mechanics.
Obviously planes could not fly unless they were serviced. For
flight attendants, their 'internal customer' was the Provision-
ing Department. The attendants could not do their jobs if the
provisions were not there.

"To show their appreciation of these internal customers,
groups would 'adopt' each other. Every quarter, they would do
something to show their appreciation. Pilots regularly showed
up at 2:00 A.M. and flipped burgers or cooked barbecue din-
ners for the mechanics who worked from 11:00 P.M. to 7:00
A.M."

According to *Inventive Incentives*, a manual the airline published for its management, it costs very little to let employees know how much they're appreciated and how valuable they are. "It can be as simple as decorating an employee's cubicle in honor of one of their life's special events," Grubbs-West remembered, "or perfect attendance lunches or a birthday cake to celebrate someone's birthday."

Grubbs-West, who taught leadership classes during her tenure at Southwest, introduced her classes to the airline's unique culture when she encouraged managers to get to know their people, one of the distinctions that continue to contribute to Southwest's unprecedented success. Southwest treats its team members as people who are more than just employee numbers. In return, employees reward it with loyalty—Southwest's turnover rate is the best in the industry.

"When I taught leadership at the University for People, we introduced an 'ancient Japanese leadership style' called GTHOOYO, demonstrating a karate chop as we chanted 'Getoyo!'" recalled Grubbs-West.

"Actually, this leadership style didn't originate in ancient Japan, but was the acronym for 'Get the Heck Out of Your Office!'—also known as Management by Walking Around and an extremely important part of Southwest's leadership philosophy."

Southwest's communication strategies have paid dividends even in the very tough times the company has faced the past several years. During the most financially challenging time in history for the airline industry, Southwest Airlines' employees voluntarily forfeited $5 million in vacation time and $1 million in pay to help the company. Employees also took over the lawn and facility maintenance at corporate headquarters. These employees were simply reflecting the deep commitment—personal and professional—that they felt from their leadership. When you lead with 100 percent commitment, and open and honest communication, this is the kind of winning spirit you can inspire.

These communication conductors—spoken, written, and demonstrated—have continued to energize Southwest Airlines and have helped propel it to its position as the nation's most consistently profitable airline.

Good Communication Begins Internally

Unfortunately, very few organizations are completely satisfied with their internal communications. No matter how many workshops are conducted, how much emphasis it's given, and how many e-mails or memos are circulated, organizations rarely have the clear communication channel that they envisioned.

However, that's no excuse to stop making an effort. It's important to *continue* making every effort to enhance your internal communications at every level of your organization.

The strength of your internal communications parallels how well you connect and communicate with your external audiences—customers, vendors, and the community. If employees are able to work seamlessly across departmental functions to provide an extraordinary customer experience, results will improve—guaranteed.

At one major corporation, leadership realized there were problems with internal communications. Departments weren't communicating well. Managers weren't all hearing the same messages during staff meetings. Yet the CEO didn't give it much thought. "People make mistakes," he reasoned. "Nobody's perfect." However, as one client after another moved their business to a competitor, the CEO began focusing his undivided attention on the bottom line, asking, "Why are we losing customers?"

The list of reasons wasn't pretty.

Deliveries were late. Service was haphazard. Dispatching was sloppy. Product reliability was suffering. In fact, during a focus group session, former clients indicated that every problem they'd experienced could be traced back to communication issues.

At the end of the meeting, the focus group facilitator summed up the results: "Your people aren't communicating well, internally or externally. Your organization appears in disarray to your clients. Processes seem chaotic. You're going to have to repair your image, for starters, and while you're doing that, you need to work on both sides of your communication, internal and external."

After much thought, the CEO began to consider the facilitator's suggestions. His first inclination was to tweak the system already in place, but then he thought better of it. Perhaps it would take more than tweaking. He called in an informal communication task force of managers, team leaders, and employees. After some discussion, he felt the task force had come up with a better strategy.

After reflecting on the communication process within his organization, the CEO determined that:

- **It matters what they hear, not what you say.** A two-way process is essential to the communication conductor. Every employee may have a different interpretation of what you say. Without a feedback mechanism, the conductor will not work.

- **It matters what they read, not what you write.** E-mail and text messaging are great communication tools for some things. However, no one can read your mind. Be crystal clear in all your communication and leave as little as possible open to interpretation.

- **If there's no trust of leadership, none of what you say or do matters anyway.**

Good Communication Means Good Listening

In 1837 Hans Christian Andersen wrote *The Emperor's New Clothes*, a classic fable. As with all fairy tales, though, the story about the vain and powerful emperor has important lessons to teach us. Believe it or not, I think this fable has several terrific leadership lessons.

You're probably familiar with Andersen's tale, but just in case you're not, I'll remind you that the gist is that the emperor goes naked in a parade because everyone is afraid to tell him the truth about his new suit. It takes a small child to point out the obvious, but by then it's much too late to fix this embarrassing situation.

The moral of the story for leaders is that we shouldn't get so caught up in our own leadership positions that we're afraid to ask for feedback. Good communication is a two-way street, and you need to listen just as much as you speak.

But more important, you must first create an atmosphere where honest feedback and suggestions are welcomed, without recourse. Does your team feel comfortable telling you the truth, or do they feel they have to tell you what you want to hear? If your team is intimidated by the power of your position or the pressure to conform to the majority, sooner or later you could also be like the emperor and get caught in an embarrassing position.

Communication in Action

During my career at FedEx, once a year every employee was asked to complete a survey that would help leadership gauge employee satisfaction or discontent. The survey was relatively simple—less than thirty questions—but designed to get to the heart of any burning issue within the work group, department, or corporation. The results were tabulated and distributed by a third party along with the recommendations for improvement.

Surveys are not unique in American organizations. What was unique about the FedEx survey was that management's bonuses were dependent upon satisfactory results from their team. If a manager's scores were not at an acceptable level, she became ineligible for a bonus. In addition, it was required that all managers conduct a feedback session that provided employees the opportunity to express why they felt the way they did—both positively and negatively. Then after the feedback session, the manager had to create a plan to address the issues raised in the survey.

The FedEx survey was more than just a survey. It was a communication strategy that began with the survey, was followed by a feedback session, and concluded with an actionable plan that managers were held accountable for implementing. Survey—feedback—action. Without the action, the survey would have been wasted time.

Asking for feedback, and really listening to what is said, is an effective way to energize your organization. If you're willing to listen, the people in your organization will usually be willing to tell you what you need to know.

Communicating Above Distractions

You'd think that with all our electronic communication devices we'd be better at actually communicating. But too often those technological marvels become nothing more than distractions. Remember when we used to complain about the telephone always ringing? I miss those simpler times! Now we have to deal with voicemail, e-mail, cell phones, PDAs, podcasts, 24-hour news channels, and text messaging—and sometimes even the telephone!

More times than we realize, these distractions cloud the

message of our communications, so what we *say* and what people *hear* are two entirely different things. Remember, some people process audio information best, while others who are more visual prefer written messages. Some people process just the words of a message, while others look for messages in body language, facial expressions, posture, clothing styles, and other subtle cues. With all these extra considerations, it's no wonder that our messages sometimes get skewed or even obscured entirely.

Whether we like it or not, the person receiving our communication decides whether our message is successful. Effective, connected communication is not about you—it's about the other person. It's not about the message that gets *transmitted*—it's about the message that gets *received*. But you can help this communication process enormously by transmitting each message accurately, consistently, simply, and effectively.

For instance, if you've ever had telephone training, someone probably encouraged you to smile when you talk on the phone. It really works—it's possible to "hear" the smile in your voice. That's a very simple beginning to successful communication.

The same care and awareness should go into every written communication. Is the message well worded? Is it free of spelling and grammatical errors? Is it spare and efficient, or did you use fifteen words when you only needed ten? Does the message convey what you want to say? Is it clear and concise?

Another key to good communication is to personalize the message. Of course, if you're sending a communication to a large group of people, that's difficult to do. But whenever possible, if you will ensure that your communication is geared to the specific audience that will be receiving it, there's a much greater chance your message will cut through all the distractions, be well received, and, most important, be understood.

And finally, don't let technology distract you from your message. You need to communicate above the distractions, so choose the best method for getting your message out. If you're e-mailing or texting a message, are you providing enough information to communicate clearly? Or is the message so short that it's confusing? Will you need to send a follow-up e-mail or two, or even schedule an audio conference call, to clear up the confusion?

Communicating Knowledge

One of the best investments of your time is to teach your team the business of your business. People have a basic need to understand how they fit into a worthwhile cause.

Maybe you've heard the story about three people working side by side on a construction job. All three people were asked the same question: "What is your job?"

The first person never looked up, but said, "My job is to do what I am told for eight hours so I can get a check."

The second person replied, "My job is to crush rocks, and I am a great rock crusher."

The third person looked up and said with pride, "My job is to build a cathedral."

Three people—all doing the same job, but with completely different perspectives. Which of the three do you think would be the best long-term employee? Although the first person can perform many tasks and the second can crush rocks for other projects, the third person will likely be the most committed. The odds are he will have a greater sense of job satisfaction because he understands his purpose and how he fits into the big picture.

Learning creates energy. You can create a strategic advantage for your organization by providing resources for your team members to learn and share knowledge. Knowledge shared is energy multiplied because it's contagious.

IBM learned long ago that an educated workforce creates energy, so the company's training goes far beyond the training department. They have unleashed knowledge by giving their employees the resources—books, classes paid for by IBM, online subscriptions—to learn on their own. The IBM philosophy is to provide every employee the opportunity to create a thirst for continuous growth. When people are learning, they grow, and when they are growing, the organization prospers!

Teach the Business of Your Business

Ritz-Carlton is one of the best known and finest hotel chains in the world. Customer service is more than just a slogan for this company—it's a unique way of doing business. One reason Ritz-Carlton is consistently among the highest-rated hotels is because of the way its managers communicate with their employees. They operate in an "open kimono" management philosophy—everything is shared with their employees.

Before every shift, teams meet for ten minutes to share

critical information. Each employee receives a small packet with the day's vital information: projected hotel occupancy, a list of VIP guests and their preferences, special conference/meeting needs, and a motivational principle of the day. These brief meetings eliminate confusion and ensure that everyone knows how she impacts each customer's satisfaction. Everyone is on the same page every day.

Sharing knowledge and teaching employees the business of the business helps build understanding. The more information leaders share about the *why* behind what they are trying to accomplish, the more energized the organization becomes.

Most of the time, the people on the team already know how to solve any organizational problem—you just need to ask them. When you listen with the intent to act on their suggestions, you create energy.

Another highly successful hotel leader, Bill Marriott, believes the seven most important words a leader can say are: "I don't know . . . what do you think?"

Peter Drucker once said that everyone in an organization should know the answer to these two questions: "What is our business?" and "How is business?"

Those are some great questions —I don't know . . . what do you think? What is our business? How is business?—and most employees would love to answer them.

The 95/5 Rule

Most organizations inadvertently operate under the "95/5" rule, meaning that work groups understand about 95 percent of what goes on inside their own departments, but only 5 percent of what goes on in other parts of the organization.

Only 5 percent? Doesn't it seem they should know more about other parts of the organization? Wouldn't things work better if the team could see the big picture? You'll create energy in your organization if you "tear down the walls" between departments and show teams how each discipline contributes to the organization.

One organization tears down the walls by periodically holding an Employee Awareness Week, during which every department conducts a workshop to communicate what it does and how it fits into the big picture. At the end of the week, the entire company is energized because everyone understands how other teams contribute to the organization's success. Increasing the 5 percent to 10 or 20 percent can have an incredible impact on your team's productivity and the organization's results.

Shared knowledge creates positive energy.

Energy Multiplied

In July 2006, Comcast introduced a radical training process for customer service agents called Comcast Bullseye, an on-demand, targeted learning program to train customer service reps both professionally and personally. The program has been instrumental in helping the company to meet its business objectives through performance and process improvement.

What makes Bullseye unique is that it's available on demand, meaning there are no formal beginning or ending dates. The program has three stages:

First, new customer service reps complete a baseline assessment of their knowledge.

Then the Comcast facilitators, who take on the role of performance coaches, use these assessments to tailor a training program and to know where to direct each new employee for more training. Depending on what they need to know, employees are directed to online learning, Web sites, performance-support systems, or internal knowledge bases.

The performance coaches are a vital part of the training. They direct employees to various resources, but they're no longer the only source of information. The coach's job is to build a community of knowledge that can be shared throughout the entire organization. Learners also complete hands-on lab work, working with the company billing system and role-playing with peers.

The third phase of the training, BITS (Bringing It Together), is an integration phase where the new employees integrate all their learning into a complex working environment. New employees role-play customer interactions and demonstrate all the skills they've learned.

Comcast has found a way to multiply energy and to share knowledge throughout their organization. The result is that the customer service agents understand much more than customer service. They understand the business of Comcast and the effect they have on Comcast's success.

Making Communications Count

George Lowe, vice president of operations at Fallbrook Technologies, is widely recognized as one of the leading authorities of effective corporate communications. His philosophy is simple:

1. Make sure that every communication delivered has crystal clear objectives and is designed to create action, convey key information, or reinforce others' thinking.

2. The goal of your communication is to increase effectiveness and productivity or decrease workload and stress. If it does not accomplish one of those objectives, you do not need to be sending out the communication.

3. Any communication you touch, you own. Senders are primarily responsible for the effectiveness of the communication. Receivers are responsible for identifying problems—it is not okay to ignore items that you don't understand. Leadership is responsible for systemic issues and availability of common information.

4. Go slow to go fast—take your time to make sure the communication is right the first time.

Positive Communications

The number one item on most employees' wish list is to be appreciated for the job they do. That's right—above money, interesting work, promotions—just appreciate me for my hard work! If you do not show your team that you care, they will make the assumption that you don't care and the energy motivation will be squeezed out of your team.

McKesson Corporation is the oldest and largest health care services and information technology company in North America. During a recent regional meeting, Vice President David Evangelista invited an outside facilitator to conduct a workshop on how to develop new habits that would help motivate and engage his team. In the fast-paced health care industry, things move so quickly that they were not following through on taking care of some issues. The team's perception was that there was very little effort made to communicate positive performance.

During the workshop, the team made two groundbreaking commitments. First, to address the follow-through issue, the team created a mantra, "Think Complete." Think Complete helps the team members remember to slow down, think, and follow through. They were to ensure that the customer was satisfied before they left the job.

Second, they instituted a Team Champion program. The champion's mission is to identify, recognize, and report any positive interaction that he sees on the team. Each team has designated a member to "watch and capture" times when he sees people doing things that make a positive difference for the rest of the team and then report those recognition moments to the rest of the team.

The result has been that Think Complete has created a new mind-set for the team. The Team Champion program has generated open and honest feedback with staff members. In addition, new creative ideas for project management and processes have been generated by the work group. This simple change to paying detailed attention has led to an improvement in the organization's employee and customer satisfaction.

Energizing Mondays

As I mentioned earlier, Monday is the most important day for your team and organization because it sets the tone for the entire week. One great way to get each week started with positive energy is to make Monday your day for organization-wide learning and development. Once you have completed *Monday Morning Motivation*, choose another book—perhaps *Monday Morning Choices*—and keep the energy flowing. Let team members suggest books they're interested in or that pertain to specific issues your team or organization are currently facing. This process facilitates learning and the sharing of knowledge throughout the organization. Don't be surprised to discover that the more people learn, the more energized they become at work.

The Communication Conductor Summary

Good communication can be a powerful way to energize your organization from the top down and to connect your employees to your customers.

But good communication doesn't just happen—it takes a willingness to always seek improvements to the communication process. To improve communication within your organization, let employees know they're appreciated, tell them you want their feedback, and then actually listen to their feedback. Communication is a two-way process. Make sure you communicate above the distractions—technological and otherwise—to ensure the message you're sending to your team is the message they're receiving.

Finally, continue to create energy by communicating knowledge about the business and by promoting a culture of learning.

The Communication Conductor

- If there is no trust, it doesn't matter what you communicate.

- Don't get so caught up in your leadership position that you're afraid to ask for honest, candid feedback.

- Effective communication is not about you—it's about them!

- Knowledge shared is energy multiplied.

- Ask the three magic questions: "I don't know . . . what do you think?" "What business are we in?" and "How is business?"

- The more people learn, the more energized they become at work.

Monday Morning Discussion Questions

- How often do you ask your team for feedback and input? Do you receive it constructively and genuinely listen to their ideas?

- Do you promote a culture of learning within your team? What additional information and knowledge can you share with team members so they will better understand the business of your business?

- How can you tear down walls and create better connections within your team? Between your team and others in the organization?

Three Things You Will Do This Week to Improve Communication

1. ———————————————————

2. ———————————————————

3. ———————————————————

7

Customer Passion

Sometimes one pays the most for the things one gets for nothing.
—ALBERT EINSTEIN

Since the first pair of shoes was sold, the art of selling shoes has always been a high-touch market. Naturally, people want to know how the shoe fits and feels as well has how it looks on them. So how can you use the power of the Internet to duplicate that experience when the customer may live many thousands of miles away from the "store"?

Zappos.com addressed that question and has been one of America's greatest success stories in recent years. Founded in 1999, Zappos.com has become a billion-dollar company selling shoes, clothing, and handbags exclusively over the Internet. The company's business was created because, according to Zappos research, only one out of three customers who go to a store to buy shoes are able to find the size and color they are looking for.

Zappos stocks more than three million pairs of shoes and claims to offer the best selection and service of any shoe store in the world. Its philosophy is that people will buy from the company with the best service and best selection and Zappos. com will be that company.

If you visit its Web site, you will discover that its self-service site creates a fabulous, friction-free customer experience—contrary to the automated service provided by so many online and traditional catalog retailers. The company understands its customers' needs, what information customers need to make a purchase, and how customer recommendations can build and reinforce a sense of community and commitment. Zappos constantly gathers feedback from customers that, in turn, makes the site more useful to more people. It's an online experience that somehow feels human.

Zappos's philosophy is to provide—through the Web site and phone service—the same high-touch service that you expect in a physical shoe store. Its entire business is built around becoming the online service leader. The company offers free shipping on orders as well as on returns if a shoe does not fit perfectly, and you can return any purchase within 365 days. Customer service reps have the authority to make any decision necessary to take care of their customer.

What is the secret to Zappos's success? Employee training and customer passion. Every Zappos employee knows shoes and loves shoes or they do not work at Zappos! Once he or she is hired, the new employee is cross-trained in every aspect of the organization. For example, every new employee hired in the corporate office is required to work in customer loyalty training (answering phones in the call center) for four weeks before they begin the job they were hired to do. By investing in this training, every person in corporate headquarters understands what is required to take care of their customers.

In addition, Zappos does a great job of building loyal, passionate customers. First, it offers a huge selection. Second, it offers unparalleled service. And third, it involves customers in the process by encouraging them to provide feedback and commentary to the site and to give Zappos advice on how the company can make its service even better.

Zappos has figured out that making connections with your customers will energize your entire organization, and it will also allow you to meet and exceed customer expectations. The result? It is consistently rated one of the top service-oriented companies in the country.

The Power of the Customer Passion Conductor

Most customers aren't unreasonable—but they do have needs. They need to be listened to, paid attention to, and treated with respect. And if you can eliminate hassle and stress from their decisions, customers will become loyal to your organization. Focusing on the customer creates long-term customer loyalty, which will energize your entire organization and ensure lasting organizational success. Can you name any organization that gets positive referrals from *un*happy customers? In fact, even just a few unhappy customers can tremendously affect your bottom line because they tend to be very loud, very opinionated, and very public in their dissatisfaction.

Every organization wants new customers. A new customer creates energy and is a positive event. However, the energy a new customer creates cannot begin to compensate for the energy that is lost when unhappy customers move on to a competitor. Even if you're gaining five customers a week, if you're losing another five, you're on a downward spiral.

You may think that you are breaking even when you lose five customers while gaining five customers, but you are really losing. Why? Because an unhappy customer who defects will tell an average of sixteen people why he was dissatisfied with your service. The new customer might tell an average of two people why he is satisfied—if you're lucky.

That's why it's so crucial for your team to be passionate about your customers, identify their needs, connect with them, and keep them happy. Customer Passion is vital in generating day-to day energy and in sustaining energy as your business grows.

Loyal customers create more powerful energy than new customers. Loyal customers are proof that whatever you're doing, you're doing it right! Let's look at how focusing on retaining loyal customers can make a difference over time.

Let's imagine two customer-focused companies, A and B, which compete in the same industry. Each has one hundred customers and each is adding new customers at a rate of 15 percent per year. By working extra hard to keep its customers happy, Company A retains 95 percent of its customers each year, while Company B retains 90 percent. That 5 percent doesn't sound like a big difference, does it? However, that small difference will compound over time to result in a large difference. You can see the impact of customer retention below:

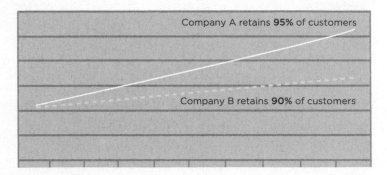

Even though both companies are adding 15 percent more customers each year, because Company A has retained 5 percent more customers each year, after ten years Company A has 60 percent more customers.

There is no escaping it—the Customer Passion conductor has a direct impact on your bottom line!

Customer Passion Begins with Your Team

If your customers are unhappy, you'll eventually end up with unhappy employees too. If your employees are unhappy, your customers will be unhappy as well . . . it becomes a vicious cycle. Constant customer complaints can sap the energy from your organization faster than almost anything. If the customer is always right, and they're always complaining, why would your employees want to stick with you? Who wants to listen to customers complain all day?

But happy customers energize employees. Everybody wants to work for the best!

Let's take another look at Southwest Airlines. If you've ever flown Southwest, you know the flight attendants, gate agents, and pilots are some of the nicest and friendliest in the business. Most Southwest employees enjoy smiling and creating an environment where their customers smile and even laugh. Compare that with other airline experiences. When customers are around employees who are proud of their organization, energy is increased. The front line employee becomes an energy conductor.

However, in any company, dissatisfied customers and dissatisfied employees become ill-will ambassadors who affect the organization's reputation. I was reminded of how true that is on a recent weekend trip when we stopped to buy ice cream. When we entered the shop, the employees didn't seem to even notice us. They never smiled and never made eye contact, and, after a while, we felt almost apologetic for ordering our ice cream cones. Obviously, those employees were neither happy to be there that day nor proud to work for that employer. We'll probably never stop there again. Without even meaning to, the unhappy employees became ill-will ambassadors. They sapped the energy from us and ended up creating not only dissatisfied customers but also more ill-will ambassadors.

Give Me Lagniappe

"Lagniappe" (lan-yap) may be a new term to you, but it is an important term to your customer. Let me explain. Lagniappe is a French word that means "a little something extra or an unexpected gift." Many years ago in Louisiana, French Creole store owners used lagniappe as a reward to attract and keep their customers. For example, if a customer ordered five pounds of sugar, the clerk would dish out five pounds on the scale and then, with a smile, add an additional measure and say "lagniappe." That was the store owner's way of adding a little extra value and saying "your business is important!"

Basically, these store owners were underpromising and overdelivering. Who knows? Maybe that extra measure was actually rolled into the price, but the customer's perception was they were receiving a little something extra. And customers saw in the eyes of store owners that their business was appreciated. How could customers not smile back when store owners had just given them more than their expectations and had smiled while uttering the word "lagniappe"?

Don't you think these customers walked away feeling good about doing business with the Creole shopkeepers? You bet they did! Customers enjoy positive surprises. In fact, my most memorable experiences, good and bad, are things that happened randomly and unexpectedly. Who doesn't enjoy receiving a little something over and above his or her expectations? Who doesn't appreciate a little extra help? And the customer rule of reciprocity is this: "When I enjoy doing business with you, I will spend more money with you."

Lagniappe creation is a pretty simple strategy for customer service success, isn't it? Deliver what you promise—add a little something extra, make the customer's experience enjoyable, and they will spend more money with you.

But here's the catch: Before lagniappe can be added, you have to understand what your customers expect from you—it is hard to give more than expected when you do not know what is expected.

Think about the experience of filling a prescription. In the past, you would go to the local drugstore, turn in your prescription, carry on a conversation with the pharmacist, and walk away with your medicine. That was what you expected, received, and were willing to pay for. The lagniappe was the personal interaction.

Today, not many pharmacists are available to carry on personal conversations. Your choices are different. You can go to the nearby chain drugstore, stand in line for twenty minutes, and you're usually ignored and rarely even recognized. You become frustrated, turn in the prescription, and wait another twenty minutes for the medicine. Or, without leaving your house, you can call or go online with a drug company, submit your order using your telephone buttons or keyboard, and have three months supply of your medicine delivered to your house the next day.

Without a relationship with your pharmacist, there is really no good reason to keep doing business the traditional way. The value that personalized customer service should be adding is actually preventing a pleasant experience because there is no established relationship. Instead of lagniappe, customers receive less and less of what they expect.

Most of our customers' expectations are fair: be passionate about serving them, understand their expectations, deliver your promises, and add lagniappe.

Adding lagniappe doesn't have to be clever, expensive, or time-consuming. Just add a little something extra. Here are some examples of organizations that are adding lagniappe to their customer's experience:

> **Southwest Airlines**—donuts and coffee;
> **Marriott Hotels**—juice and fruit;
> **Olive Garden**—breadsticks;
> **Lands' End**—no-questions-asked return policy;
> **Doubletree Hotels**—warm cookies upon arrival;
> **Lexus**—return cars sparkling clean after routine service;
> **Discount Tire**—tires rotated and flats fixed for free;
> **Real Estate Agent**—carpets cleaned for free when house is listed for sale;
> **Wal-Mart**—personal greeting at every door;
> **Nordstrom**—personalized cards sent to customers;
> **O'Reilly Auto**—wiper blades changed for free.

Customer Passion Conductor ROI

The best news is that the Customer Passion conductor has a direct return on investment. Loyal customers are created primarily through outstanding customer connections. People choose to become customers for many different reasons—perhaps because of new product ideas, your ingenious marketing campaigns, or your company's reputation. However, in most instances, the real "magic" can be found in how well you have connected with your customer.

It's been shown that customers continue to do business with an organization because of the service they receive. Studies have shown customers defect for reasons that seldom have anything to do with product quality. In fact, most customers leave because they feel the chilly air of indifference—as we did in the ice-cream store. The customer who doesn't feel a connection has less reason to return.

Even if you're selling the finest product of its kind, good customers will eventually disappear if a positive connection is missing. Customers need a positive connection.

More Than Talk . . . Walk the Talk!

Every organization talks about focusing on the customer—the slogans blanket the halls of almost every company. These may sound familiar:

- Customers Are First!
- We Exist to Serve the Customer!
- Think Customer!
- Customer Champions!
- 100% Customer-Focused!
- The Customer Is King!
- We Are Customer-Driven!

Though the slogans are nice and make great banners and T-shirts, many customers will tell you that in many organizations "customer service" is a contradictory phrase—an oxymoron.

The good news? It doesn't have to be that way!

In fact, improving customer service really comes down to doing a few things extremely well. It begins when the Customer Passion conductor is in place and working both ways, connecting customer needs with your organization's objectives, and solving the customer's problems with your organization's products and services.

Second-Mile Service

Chick-fil-A is an incredible success story. Even though the company's stores are only open six days a week—one of its core values is to allow all employees to spend Sunday with family—Chick-fil-A is highly successful in the intensely competitive fast food industry.

Truett Cathy, founder of Chick-fil-A, introduced three energizing words to his team: "It's my pleasure."

It's a very simple technique. Whenever you request something, a Chick-fil-A associate always responds, "It's my pleasure." But—and here's the magic ingredient—the energy doesn't come from the voice or the words. It's in the attitude. At Chick-fil-A, they've created an environment where it truly *is* a pleasure to serve their customers. The organization spends a considerable amount of time attracting employees who really desire to serve the customer.

Chick-fil-A practices what it calls "second-mile service." A clean restroom is first-mile service—everyone in the industry can do that. Second-mile service is going beyond what everyone else does and going the extra mile. At Chick-fil-A, it's not unusual to see employees helping someone to the car in the rain, carrying a tray for a mom who has young kids in tow, or picking up wastepaper while conversing with diners. Each of those experiences exhibits second-mile service and allows energy to flow between the customer and employee.

Chick-fil-A is focused on the customer and those who serve the customer. Every Chick-fil-A store bears a plaque engraved with this principle: "Associate yourselves only with those people you can be proud of—whether they work for you or you work for them." Cathy realized early in his business career that if you take care of your people, they will take care of the customers.

The Silent but Deadly Customer

How much attention does your organization pay to customer satisfaction? Unfortunately, you can't depend on your customers to provide the feedback you need to conduct energy.

Here's why: There are many types of customers. Some are so nice that you never hear from them, others are always complaining, and still others are somewhere in between. Regardless of how you classify your customers, don't take any of them for granted.

Unfortunately, your "nice" customers can absolutely kill your business. They're so nice that they never complain—so you assume everything is okay. Eventually, many of those nice customers become ex-customers.

In fact, studies show only 4 percent of your customers will take time to complain. The ones who do not complain assume nothing will change anyway, so who needs the hassle? Sometimes your nice customers will consider raising an issue so they'll feel better, but it's easier to just leave quietly. Again, who needs the hassle? These customers don't bother to invest the energy in complaining because they know they're never coming back—and can you blame them?

So how can you measure and monitor your customer connections?

Absolutely, Positively, Passionately Connected!

Many organizations measure the percentage of satisfied customers. Most of these organizations are happy with 95 percent customer satisfaction. At FedEx, 95 percent wasn't good enough, and neither was 99 percent. Ninety-five percent customer satisfaction means that 150,000 FedEx customers would be dissatisfied—every day. Can you imagine dealing with 150,000 dissatisfied customers every day? Customer satisfaction is not only a passion of FedEx, but also a business necessity.

FedEx was experiencing tremendous growth in the early 1990s. Business was good, which created plenty of opportunities to overlook disappointed customers. New customers were coming on board faster than the ones the company lost. However, FedEx was passionate about customer satisfaction. To ensure accountability throughout the organization, FedEx established two groundbreaking customer service initiatives.

1. Jim Barksdale, former COO of FedEx, created a customer service philosophy that every package should be treated as the customer's golden package—the package that could make or break that customer's business.

Out of the millions of packages FedEx picked up, sorted, and delivered, FedEx employees were to treat every one as though it were the most important package in the world. That "golden package" mind-set was a significant factor in FedEx becoming one of the most reliable service companies in the world. The mind-set change from delivering packages to delivering golden packages resonated with every person responsible for handling every package. Those packages were golden!

2. FedEx abandoned its measurement of on-time deliveries and replaced it with an index that described how its performance was viewed by customers. FedEx identified, weighed, and monitored every factor that could go wrong in its connection with customers.

Fred Smith, CEO of FedEx, called these potential customer disconnections the "hierarchy of horrors." His philosophy? While all customer disconnections are bad, the worst ones need to be monitored and addressed in accordance with the severity of the disconnection.

For instance, a package delivered at 10:32 A.M. was a service failure because it did not meet the commitment time of

10:30 A.M. Any package delivered late was a service failure, but a delivery that was late by minutes was not as damaging to the customer as a delivery that was late by a day or more—that was a service disaster.

To measure and monitor its service connection, FedEx created the Service Quality Indicator (SQI) to identify each type of service failure, and then assigned a value to each one based on its impact on customer satisfaction. For example, the three most severe service failures (damaged packages, lost packages, and missed pickups) were assigned a value of 10 in the SQI, while less serious problems were weighted either 5 or 1.

Every day, the SQI was monitored and service adjustments quickly made. Most adjustments were to the system and didn't involve people. However, any time performance standards were not met, the specific employee, station, or department was identified, held accountable, and was responsible for rapid improvement.

The result? A year after introducing the SQI, service failures were down 11 percent while package volume was up 20 percent! Thanks in large part to the SQI and its resulting service improvements, in 1990 FedEx became the first service company to win the Malcolm Baldrige National Quality Award.

FedEx is considered one of the most reliable companies in its industry because it doesn't measure the service connection by its own internal standards—it defines and measures it from the customer's perspective.

Every organization can duplicate the FedEx model of the customer connection by following these key steps:

1. Create a "golden package" visual so that every person in your organization will understand the importance of creating customer satisfaction.
2. Identify your "hierarchy of horrors." What are the worst things that can happen in your customer interactions?
3. Develop a weighting system to bring attention to the service connections that create the most customer dissatisfaction.
4. Implement the necessary tools to track and monitor your service connection performance.
5. Take the necessary steps to eliminate the service connection failures.

The reason FedEx is so focused on customer satisfaction is because it knows that it takes at least a dozen positive service experiences with a customer to make up for just one bad one—that's a 12:1 ratio!

If you ignore a discontented customer, he or she will talk about the unpleasant experience—and talk about it, and talk about it some more! I'm sure all of us have heard plenty of customer service horror stories from our friends and family. If you're nodding your head in agreement right now, you've just proved my next point: angry customers always tell others about their bad experiences (their stories sometimes taking on lives of their own), and angry customers never forget.

The good news, though, is that most of the people who complain will do business with you again *if* you listen to them and personally address their complaint, quickly and efficiently.

In fact, opportunities to win loyal customers are sometimes cleverly disguised as a customer complaint. If you address your customer's issues quickly and efficiently, your customer will reward you with his or her loyalty.

When it comes to connecting with customers and earning a customer's loyalty, *everything* counts. The Customer Passion conductor begins when the customer calls on the phone, enters your Web site, or walks in the door—and it never ends!

Ensuring the Customer Passion Conductor Is a Positive Experience

Most customers don't expect you to do the impossible. They're not expecting miracles—they just want you to follow through and do what you promise.

While you're trying to make a connection with customers, you may need to work doubly hard to maintain an intense customer focus that keeps you at least one step ahead of them, anticipating their needs, so that you can quickly provide them with a product that they don't even know they need.

At Cirque du Soleil headquarters in Montreal, Quebec, every office looks out into the area where performers train and perfect their acts. This way every employee can see the organization's product in development.

Founded in 1984 by two street performers, Cirque du Soleil is a modern circus that emphasizes human performance, colorful costumes, a mixture of musical styles, and an imaginary language that, strangely, is understood everywhere in the world.

By any measure, Cirque du Soleil is an entertainment juggernaut, selling about seven million tickets annually that generate an estimated revenue of more than $600 million. Performances are booked three years in advance. In addition, Cirque has spun off several businesses and touring performance companies. The global impact of its brand, according to Interbrand, ranks ahead of McDonald's, Microsoft, and Disney.

Cirque's success is the result of its laser-sharp focus on adult customers who are willing to pay $100 or more for a performance. To ensure those customers see performances they'll never forget, the company hires the very best talent in the industry and every year plows more than 70 percent of its profits back into increasingly innovative projects. Its investments in people and future productions are made with the intention of delivering spectacular shows that customers will rave about long after the performance is over.

Being the Very Best

The reward for being the very best as opposed to being average is heavily skewed. People like to work for the best, buy from the best, and deal with the best . . . in almost every way in our society. The best-selling books sell millions more copies than the average book. The best movies generate millions more dollars than the average film. In almost every situation, the best in any industry is rewarded disproportionately to the average in that industry. Winners win because customers love a winner.

The rewards for being the best Customer Passion organization in your industry are enormous. Energy is created when customers flock to the winners. It is your choice to provide an atmosphere where your employees choose to deliver impeccable service that separates your organization from the average.

Customer Passion Conductor Summary

A U.S. Office of Consumer Affairs study discovered that for every unsatisfied customer who complains, twenty-six other unhappy customers say nothing. And of those twenty-six, twenty-four will not come back to do business with you.

Of the customers who register a complaint, between 54 and 70 percent will do business again with the organization if their complaints are resolved. That figure goes up to a staggering 95 percent if customers feel complaints are resolved quickly.

Unfortunately, many of your customers will walk away from doing business with your company without saying a word. In fact, on average, United States corporations lose almost half of their customers every five years. In addition, U.S. companies will lose half of their employees in four years. Coincidence? Maybe . . . but probably not!

A better answer may be that customer loyalty begins with employee loyalty. Loyal customers are the result of years spent building relationships. If employee turnover is so rampant in your organization that relationships cannot be built with your customers, you can expect to continue to see customers walk away.

It's crucial to focus on your customers' needs, connect with them, and keep them happy. Customers want a connection with those they do business with—even the finest product will not keep them coming back if they don't feel a connection.

An unhappy customer who defects will tell an average of sixteen people why he was dissatisfied with your service. The new customer might tell an average of two people why he is satisfied—if you're lucky. Unhappy customers also create unhappy employees—who wants to listen to customers complain all day?

Unhappy customers sap energy from your organization. But keeping a laser-sharp Customer Passion conductor will generate day-to-day energy and will sustain energy as your business grows.

Customer Passion Conductor

- If your customers are unhappy, you will eventually end up with unhappy employees too.

- Happy customers energize employees.

- Dissatisfied customers and dissatisfied employees become ill-will ambassadors for your organization.

- If you take care of your people, they will take care of your customers.

- Opportunities to win loyal customers are sometimes cleverly disguised as a customer complaint.

- Angry customers have elephant-like memories—they never forget!

Monday Morning Discussion Questions

- What are you currently doing to connect in a positive manner with your internal and external customers? Where can you provide "second-mile service"?

- How can you take better care of your people so they can take better care of your customers?

- What needs do you anticipate your customers (internal and external) will have in the next three years?

- What can you do to ensure that positive customer service stories are shared with all team members and employees, thereby increasing their energy?

Three Things You Will Do This Week to Create Better Customer Connections

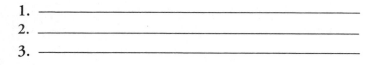

1. _____
2. _____
3. _____

8

Integrity

Anyone who doesn't take truth seriously in small matters
cannot be trusted in large ones either.
— ALBERT EINSTEIN

Integrity is the cornerstone of leadership. In our Leadership Energy Equation, you can think of integrity as the master switch that controls every other part of the equation. If your organization's leadership lacks integrity, the energy will simply stop flowing through the organization. But when integrity is intact, all the parts of the equation will work.

One of the toughest things for a leader to figure out is "What's the truth?" Many times the truth is camouflaged by politics, personal agendas, or even a sincere, intense desire to want something else to be the truth.

Leaders who search for the truth possess one of the most respected virtues in all of life—integrity. If you are truly a person who searches for the truth, regardless of politics and personal agendas, you are fast becoming a unique and valued person.

> *Weakness of attitude becomes weakness of character.*
> —ALBERT EINSTEIN

What Is Integrity?

Many people have a difficult time defining integrity—they know it when they see it—but it is tough to describe. In fact, in 2005, integrity was the single most searched for word on Merriam-Webster's dictionary Web site, which implies that a lot of people are not exactly sure what integrity means. Everyone knows that it is important to be a person of integrity, but most do not know what the word actually means.

The dictionary says integrity is the rigid adherence to a code of behavior that can be measured only by a person's actions. Your spouse may say integrity is total commitment and loyalty. Your team may say integrity is doing what you say you'll do. Your investors may define integrity as finding no surprises in your financials. Your friends probably say it is just being who you are.

To me, integrity means never being ashamed of your reflection. If you can look in the mirror every day without regret, your integrity is in check.

When I was growing up, my parents were real clear about the importance of integrity. They taught me that the worst thing I could ever lose was my reputation. In our house, we never had to define integrity; we just had to define what we thought was the right thing to do. In fact, every time I brought an issue to my dad, the first question he would ask me was "Son, what do you think is the right thing to do?" I hated that question at the time, but upon many years of reflection, I have come to realize that answering that question clarified and cemented the action I needed to take.

Where would some of the huge organizations that have fallen because of integrity issues be today if someone had answered the question "What is the right thing to do?" Would Enron's path have led to destruction, or would they still be an inspirational success story? Would WorldCom or Arthur Andersen still have thousands on their payrolls? Would Bernie Madoff have swindled over 14,000 clients for over $50 billion dollars if someone within his organization had the nerve to ask him, "Are we doing the right thing?" Would the financial meltdown of subprime mortgages have happened if the borrower, lender, underwriter, or anyone else would have asked and answered the question "What is the right thing to do?" Of course not.

What is the right thing to do? Answer that question and everything else has a good chance of falling into place.

Regardless of its definition and who describes it, integrity is a by-product of trust, which in turn is a by-product of truth and honesty. A deficit in trust can potentially cost your organization millions of dollars in sales and profits. If people are to willingly follow someone, they have to be assured that the person they are following is worthy of their trust. When people lose faith and trust in their leaders, everything else goes with it: productivity, job satisfaction, morale, and pride. Loss of trust will completely sap the energy from the organization, and it's unlikely that the energy can ever be restored.

Trust Matters

It's said that people routinely question the truth of about 50 percent of everything they read. Why? Because experience has taught them how often they encounter exaggerations, white lies, and outright untruths. Almost every day, and in every type of situation, they see a trail of broken promises, unmet commitments, and overstated facts. They're starting to wonder who they can believe these days. Can they believe you?

Honesty, not technique, is the secret to good communication. Trust comes before technique. You may have the technique, but if you don't keep your promises and take care of business, all the technique in the world won't make you a good communicator. Brian Tracy, a friend and best-selling author of personal development books, once said, "The glue that holds all relationships together—including the relationship between the leader and the led—is trust, and trust is based on integrity."

Working with people in organizations is much like being in a marriage. Honesty and trust are the basic foundation for any successful relationship—between colleagues, with customers, or among friends. Relationships are built and sustained on trust. If the trust is broken, some relationships cannot be mended. Trust is the glue!

Marianne M. Jennings is a professor of legal and ethical

studies in business at Arizona State University. In a recent article, she writes, "There is a circle of trust in the capitalistic economy, and to the extent that the conductor of trust is lost, there will be a breakdown in the free enterprise system that affords opportunity for individual achievement." Powerful words with an even more powerful message: Without trust, entire economies and systems can fail. There is no energy without trust.

In her article "Honesty in Business," Jennings cites a study ("Honesty and Survivor Management") by Professor Frank Shipper, a management expert at Salisbury University in Maryland. Shipper wondered why some managers had survived numerous corporate downsizings while their peers had not.

He found that although the surviving managers were highly diverse in terms of gender, age, race, and management style, all had one characteristic in common: both they and their employees described them as *honest*. They gave credit to their employees when due, used candor in their dealings with others, and consistently practiced kindness and fairness. Shipper found that these managers enjoyed job security and success *because* of these qualities, not despite them.

Be Prepared to Be Honest

Business practices are more transparent today than at any time in history. Because so many once-lauded organizations were found to be morally destitute in the early part of this decade, the Sarbanes-Oxley legislation and other measures make it imperative for organizations and individuals to be honest . . . period.

In *Chalk*, a movie about the trials and tribulations of high school teachers, the teachers are filmed at a meeting where they're asked such penetrating questions as: "How many of you have taken home a stapler that belonged to the school? How many have used a ream of paper to make fliers for your personal weekend garage sales? How many of you have borrowed money from your organizational fund-raiser to buy a round of beer on Friday afternoon?"

Sadly, by the time all the questions had been asked, many teachers were guiltily looking at their feet.

Staplers and paper seem like such small things, but personal honesty is the basis of the corporate image. If Cynthia laughs about charging a personal dinner on the corporate credit card, then what will her customer think about the integrity of that business?

Improper charges on expense reports are symptomatic of a bigger problem with ethics. And if a company's ethics are questionable, depletion of its energy can't be far behind.

After the demise of Enron, Arthur Andersen, and World-Com, organizations that understood the importance of integrity began developing a culture that demands honesty, ethical behavior, and more transparency, and punishes those who fall short of the standard. When organizations have zero tolerance for dishonesty or unethical behavior, their brands and their images survive. These companies will ultimately win competitive battles because their customers know without a doubt who they are, what they are, and where they are headed.

For organizations and individuals, it's not enough just to be honest anymore. Transparency is just as crucial. Transparent organizations and people are those who share information proactively, freely, and in a timely manner, rather than reactively when asked for it. In other words, they are willing to freely share with others not only what their "talk" is, but also how well they walk that talk. Not showing what you're doing is simply not accepted anymore. Honesty, integrity, and transparency are inextricably linked.

Unconditional Integrity

Organizational integrity is not something that changes based on forecasted quarterly earnings. It isn't determined by what it takes to make the next sale or for political staging at an upcoming board meeting. Organizational integrity is consistent regardless of the internal and external factors that may be swirling around the organization.

Con-way is one of the leading transportation companies in America. Founded in 1983, Con-way is widely considered to be a world-class organization. Its success did not come overnight; it was earned by creating and implementing a dedicated strategy focusing on customer satisfaction, employee engagement, and strong adherence to its corporate values.

In 1998, Con-way established a corporate constitution that would become the anchor of how the company would conduct business. The constitution consisted of three parts: a formal employee recognition program, a new mission statement, and a definition of the organization's operating values.

The first of the three anchors, the formal employee recognition program, was created to recognize values-driven performance at all levels within the organization. It consisted of four levels of recognition:

- Star Cards: Small note-type cards with envelopes presented *by* anyone *to* anyone when outstanding values-driven behavior is exhibited.

- Quarterly Leader Award: Through a nomination process, employees propose one another for this recognition. A small number of employees are selected each quarter and presented with a crystal award.

- President's Award: From the quarterly winners, the compamy's president selects a small number of employees who exhibited outstanding values leadership. A festive celebration and presentation banquet event with spouses or special guests is held.

- CEO Constellation Award: Honors the "best of the best" and is the highest and most prestigious award a member of the Con-way organization can receive.

The President's Award and the Constellation Award are the most prestigious as well as the most expensive awards for Con-way. When economic conditions are good, it is easy to celebrate individual achievements with formal recognition—regardless of the cost. What about when times are tough? What about when you are moving through uncharted times? Should you disband the constitution and send the message that it was a conditional constitution—that rewards should be expected only when the company exceeds plan regardless of individual performance?

Con-way, like almost every other organization in America, had to answer those questions. It ultimately came down, once again, to the basic integrity question: "What is the right thing to do?" Con-way leaders decided that their constitution was not conditional . . . their integrity was not conditional . . . their expectations were not conditional . . . and therefore their recognition should remain intact, even though other sacrifices would have to be made.

Con-way spent years preparing to be a world-class organization, and world-class organizations take care of their best people regardless of the economic conditions. The company passed its integrity test even though some people took issue with the expense incurred to recognize employees in tough times.

The result of staying the course, adhering to Con-way's constitution, and continuing to recognize performance was the confidence and assurance that the company's core values were real and not conditional regardless of economic conditions.

Personal Integrity in Action

Your personal integrity is judged every day. The people in your organization judge your integrity not by what they hear you say, but by what they see you do. When you criticize one of your team members in public, you lose integrity. When you encourage your sales team to stretch the truth and say, "We'll deal with it later," your integrity comes into question. When you show favoritism, choose to not return phone calls, say you're out of the office when you're not, or say that you didn't receive a message when you did—you lose trust. Of course, you probably wouldn't intentionally do most of these things, but our intentions really don't matter. What matters is what we do. People judge your integrity on what they see—and they either see it or they don't.

Is there a time when a small, white lie is small enough that it doesn't really matter? Is there a point at which small lies are okay but big ones aren't? If so, where is that point . . . and how does your team know when they cross the line? The answer is that to protect your integrity, no lie is so small that it doesn't matter. You cannot pick and choose when you will be a person of integrity. You can't justify a white lie by thinking, "No one was hurt so it's okay." Once you start making excuses, the excuses will come a little easier each time, and soon you will find yourself on a slippery slope that can lead to disaster.

There are no varying degrees of integrity. You either have it or you don't. The day in, day out, seemingly insignificant things that you do represent the greatest opportunity for integrity erosions. As minor as a small lie may seem at the time, it has a lasting effect. People don't forget integrity mistakes. They will forgive and forget most any judgment error, but integrity mistakes are forever.

> **THE PERSONAL INTEGRITY CHECK**
>
> Are my actions in sync with our organizational
>   values?
> How would I feel if this decision was shared in the
>   news?
> Would it be perfectly okay if someone made the
>   same decision that affected me?
> Is it the right thing to do?

The Middle Management Integrity Dilemma

Middle managers sometimes find themselves faced with a thorny integrity dilemma: How do they respond when they are supposed to support and implement a decision that contradicts their personal beliefs? If they support the corporate mandate, do they sacrifice their personal integrity? Would they lose the trust of the people who depend on them?

If you find yourself faced with such a situation, first ask yourself the four personal integrity check questions. If the conflict is with your personal feelings and does not contradict any of the four questions, you can express your concerns to upper management, but it is still up to you to implement the decision. Upper management may equip you with more information to better understand their decision (although it's possible that all of the information that is available to them will never be available to you). If you then fail to implement the decision, you will lose your credibility and integrity with upper management.

If the situation is unethical, illegal, or against your personal morals, you should never sacrifice your personal integrity . . . even if it means that you have to pay a huge price. Of course, this is easier said than done when you are facing implementing an unethical decision or losing your job—but if you are dealing in illegial or unethical behaviors, you will probably eventually lose your job anyway. At Enron, everyone continued on as though nothing was wrong—and they probably convinced themselves that nothing was wrong—until Sherron Watkins stood up and said, "Is this right?" You are the one facing the mirror every morning . . . if you can't feel good about going to work because of unethical or illegal activities going on there, the worst thing you can do is to get caught up in the moment and convince yourself that what you are doing is okay.

Creating a Culture of Integrity

There are five pillars that you can uphold to create a culture of integrity. Failure to adhere to any of the five will destroy confidence and trust in your leadership.

1. *The love of truth.* A key ingredient to establishing and maintaining your integrity is to discover and then face the real truth—not what you hope to be the truth, but the absolute reality of your situation. Our nature is to be selective with the truth and cling to the things that are pleasant to us.

Jack Welch, former CEO of General Electric, calls the love of truth the "candor effect." He says that absolute candor will "unclutter" conversations because everyone will speak what is actually the truth and not the political rhetoric that goes on in many meeting rooms and boardrooms across the nation. The love of truth is an unnatural act worth doing.

Choosing to search for the truth and having the courage to confront the hard realities will make the road to success a little straighter and the challenges less overwhelming and create fewer surprises along the way.

One of the realities that you have to face is that you cannot do everything. It may sound simple, but many leaders make the mistake of overcommitting or committing to something beyond their control. Living up to your commitments is one of the principal ways your integrity is judged.

2. *Courage to stand up and speak out for what you believe.* To stand up for your beliefs, you have to know what you stand for. Your integrity begins when you speak out about what you believe. What are your core values? What's so important that it will never be compromised for any reason?

Never leave people guessing about how you feel or where you stand. Understand exactly what you believe and communicate those beliefs without hesitation. Your integrity has to be tested and proven. If you have any question about what your personal values are, how can they be tested and proven? If your beliefs and values are integrity based, they will never change.

It takes courage to take a stand. For every person, there comes a time when you must step forward and take a stand for what you feel is important.

3. *Persevere in your pursuit of fairness.* In a gray area, err on the side of fairness. What you do is being closely watched by your team, and their judgments are based on *their* perception of what they observe. It may not be fair, but you have to manage your people's perceptions—not all decisions are black or white. Err on the side of your team. Swallowing your pride is a small price to pay to retain or gain their trust in you.

4. *Live what you teach.* Talking about integrity is easy. In fact, in Enron's 2001 annual report, integrity was listed as one of its important corporate values— along with communication, respect, and excellence. It seems sort of silly now, but Enron's leaders probably spent thousands of hours identifying which values to list. The list does not mean anything—the way they ran their company meant everything.

People listen to what you say and watch the way you deliver the message, but they react to what they see you do. You can't fake what you teach. Walk your talk! The ultimate test of your integrity is whether you do what you said you'd do. Your word and your commitment are judged every time you commit to something—regardless of how insignificant you consider the commitment. When your integrity is sacrificed for any reason, recovering it won't be easy.

When you fail to treasure the truthful and forthright, you will gradually find yourself surrounded by flattering fools who conceal truths for their convenience and yours. When the stakes for saying and hearing the truth are too high, one lives a life of deceit.

5. *Continually ask, "What is the right thing to do?"*

Integrity in Action

There are thousands of organizations that are led by leaders of integrity and never make the news. It seems that only the organizations that breach their integrity are the ones who receive exposure. However, a great example of corporate integrity that was exposed for all to see was McNeil Consumer Products. The company asked and answered "What is the right thing to do?" during a period of intense pressure. Yes, you've probably heard this story before. But it is worth revisiting as a tremendous example of corporate integrity and transparency.

In the fall of 1982, seven people on the west side of Chicago mysteriously died. Investigators found that each of the victims had ingested an extra-strength Tylenol capsule before dying—capsules that were found to be laced with cyanide.

News of these incidents traveled fast, causing a massive nationwide panic. A typical corporation's response might have been to minimize the issue and start looking for others to blame for the problem. After all, it was only a few bottles and isolated in a small area of Chicago.

Officials at McNeil Consumer Products, a subsidiary of Johnson & Johnson and the makers of Tylenol, made a tough choice, one that tested their integrity. They acted quickly, immediately alerting consumers across the nation not to consume any type of Tylenol product. Then, along with halting production and any Tylenol advertising, James Burke, Johnson & Johnson's CEO, ordered the recall of approximately 31 million bottles of Tylenol with a retail value of more than $100 million.

Every major newscast focused on shelf after shelf of Tylenol products being swept into large plastic bags for disposal. It was a time of humiliation for Johnson & Johnson.

A few days later, Johnson & Johnson offered to exchange all Tylenol capsules that already had been purchased for new Tylenol tablets at a cost of several million dollars more to the corporation. Immediately thereafter, the company offered a $100,000 reward for the capture of the individual or individuals involved in the tampering case.

Without a doubt, Johnson & Johnson had put customer safety first before worrying about the company's profit and other financial concerns. It passed the integrity test. Its actions became the benchmark of corporate integrity—doing the right thing, regardless of the consequences.

Through the company's actions, it became obvious that Johnson & Johnson only wanted to do the right thing, once the link between Tylenol and the seven deaths in Chicago had been established. In addition, when the Johnson & Johnson team developed a tamper-proof cap, it gave its competitors the specifications of the cap so they could use it too. Through its actions, Johnson & Johnson's top management let the nation know that, whatever the costs, the company would choose integrity. This choice ultimately served the leadership well as it sought to reestablish the nation's confidence in the company's products.

Integrity Conductor Summary

Without a doubt, your personal integrity is your most prized possession. Each day, that integrity is tested, and you have an opportunity to prove it or lose it with every decision you make.

Business is personal. People commit themselves to other people more than to an organization. If people don't trust the messenger, they won't buy into the message. Leadership begins with the leader's integrity. Without integrity, you can't develop trust; and without trust, nothing else really matters. Trust and honesty are the keys to integrity.

Martin Luther King Jr. once said: "The ultimate measure of a man is not where he stands in moments of comfort and convenience, but where he stands in times of challenge and controversy." Our integrity is tested and revealed by the choices we make in the most challenging times. We have to know "What is the right thing to do?" Doing the right thing is not always the easiest thing—but it is always the right thing to do. Choosing to do the right thing— even when it's painful— ensures you will maintain your most precious possession throughout your personal and professional journey.

Integrity is not just being fiscally trustworthy or handling issues in an exemplary and truthful fashion. Integrity is the commitment to do what is right regardless of the circumstance—never being ashamed of your reflection. If your organization lacks integrity, the energy will stop flowing and all the other energy conductors will cease to matter.

The Integrity Conductor

- One of the toughest things for a leader to figure out is "What is the truth?"

- If you are a person who searches for the truth—regardless of politics or personal agenda—you are a unique and valued person.

- Integrity is never being ashamed of your reflection.

- There can be no positive energy without trust.

- The ultimate test of integrity is your follow-through.

Monday Morning Discussion Questions

- On a scale of one to ten (ten being the highest), how would your team members and colleagues rate your trustworthiness? How would you rate yourself?

- Do you consistently keep your promises and live up to your commitments in all areas of your life?

- Are you honest and candid in your communications with your team and with other leaders and departments?

Three Things You Will Do This Week to Model Integrity

1. _____
2. _____
3. _____

Part Three

Optimizing Your Resources

The Leader's Impact on Energy
The Final Word

9

The Leader's
Impact on Energy

In order to be an immaculate member of a flock of sheep, one must
above all be a sheep oneself.
— ALBERT EINSTEIN

Twenty-three hundred years ago, Alexander the Great led his troops across a hot and desolate plain. After eleven days of a grueling advance, he and all the soldiers were near death from thirst. They pressed on, however, into the twelfth day.

At midday, two of his scouts brought Alexander what little water they had been able to find. It hardly filled a cup. His troops stood back and watched—expecting him to drink. Instead, he poured the water into the hot sand. Without saying a word, Alexander energized his followers by providing the only things he had to give at that moment: example and inspiration.

The multiplier to Leadership Energy is YOU. *You* are the secret power that your organization has been waiting for. YOU have tremendous influence to bring about change in your organization—to harness and release its energy, to conduct and focus that energy, and to multiply it throughout the entire organization.

But where do you even begin? How do you start reenergizing your team?

It sounds simple, but you can begin by being enthusiastic—even when you don't feel like it. If you're enthusiastic, those around you will be too. Enthusiasm multiplies energy to produce positive results.

Johnny Harrell owned a service station back in the days when service was still a part of filling your gas tank. Johnny came back from a leadership conference all fired up. He'd been told that enthusiasm alone would produce better results in business. So he called his employees together and declared, "This week we're going to conduct an experiment in enthusiasm. I want you to check the oil filter of everyone who drives in here. I want you to make an enthusiastic presentation to them about what a new oil filter can do for them if they need it."

The men went to work and carried out Johnny's instructions. At the end of the week, he checked his records to see if their enthusiastic oil filter presentations had made any difference. And guess what? They'd sold 700 percent more oil filters than in the previous best week *in 15 years*.

What was the difference? His business was still in the same location with the same men offering the same thing. The difference was *enthusiasm*. Sincere enthusiasm creates energy and produces positive results even when nothing else changes. Try it!

Passion Creates Energy

Excellence comes from work that you are passionate about. Knowing what to do is certainly important, but knowing why you do it fuels your motivation . . . your passion. A strong passion enables you to find a way to achieve your goals . . . any goal. When you are passionate about your job and the impact you are making on your organization, opportunities will present themselves where others are not able to see them.

Passion exposes opportunities and ignites your pursuit of your goals. People who are passionate will see ways to fulfill their dreams that others cannot see. Those who are not passionate are blinded by their current situation and not able to see hope and encouragement in tough times.

Nestlé USA is a good example of passion exposing opportunities. As you can imagine, during the Great Depression, the coffee business was not booming. There were mountains of unused coffee beans sitting around Brazil due to the drastic drop in demand. Instead of focusing on the diminishing sales in its traditional market, Nestlé looked around and created a way to use what it had. Coffee beans were abundant, and it used the supply to create Nescafé, an instant coffee that is still one of the company's global best sellers.

Many people and organizations have experienced their greatest accomplishments immediately after going through their toughest times. I have witnessed, in my life as well as in those of many others, that our best tends to be just a short distance beyond what we fear the most. When you have your eyes wide open you will find ways to break out of your traditional way of doing things. Challenging economic times can serve as a catalyst for organizations to search for fresh opportunities, new ways of doing business, different uses for existing products, innovative distribution channels, and creative marketing strategies.

Physical Energy Creates Leadership Energy

Maybe knowing how critical you are to your organization seems a little bit overwhelming. If you're the one responsible for constantly energizing everyone else, how do you energize yourself?

It may sound obvious, but if you're lacking physical energy, you'll find it tough to increase any other kind of energy. It's difficult to be energetic and enthusiastic when you're physically out of shape. I know you've heard this before, but it's a simple truth—increasing your physical energy level may require lifestyle changes.

Seven years ago, I underwent quadruple bypass heart surgery. Although it wasn't much fun, my heart disease was a wake-up call that forced me to change my lifestyle. The results have been positive, and I've improved my health and increased my energy.

If you need to make lifestyle changes, start now. Don't wait until you're lying on a gurney awaiting surgery. Take some time to evaluate: Are you getting enough rest? What about your exercise schedule—or does one even exist? Does your diet consist mainly of quick lunches and fast food? Are you eating more meat and potatoes than fruits and vegetables?

You can also increase your personal energy by decreasing your liquor tab. Any physician will tell you that alcohol consumption actually saps your energy. You may feel a momentary buzz after a couple of cocktails or during that third glass of wine, but don't confuse that with energy—it's just the alcohol talking. Continued alcohol consumption will drain your energy.

The bottom line: If you want to increase your organization's energy, start by increasing your own energy first. Eat a healthy diet, get enough sleep, engage in regular stress-reducing exercise, and spend some time every day focusing on your spiritual self. Your body and your mind will thank you—and reward you with more stamina.

Continuous Improvement Creates Energy

The most successful leaders are those who continue to learn and improve every day. Quite simply, leaders who are not committed to personal improvement are doomed to fail. Complacency is the root of mediocrity.

The most successful leaders energize themselves by reading about successful people. They discover that others have faced challenges similar to their own and have prospered by working through them. Choose a regular time and place to read, then *do* it. Read. It's impossible to energize your organization if you don't take the time to energize yourself.

Education is what remains after one has forgotten
everything he learned in school.
—ALBERT EINSTEIN

Start off by reading a book a month—it'll change your life. More than twenty years ago, I started reading at least a book a month, and I soon discovered that learning is contagious. The more I learned, the more people around me wanted to learn. Discover it for yourself.

There are hundreds of books to help you become more productive, yet most people read less than one book a year. If you prefer a high-tech approach, download audiobooks or motivational podcasts that you can plug into during a flight. Take advantage of technology to educate and motivate yourself professionally, personally, and spiritually, and you'll take control of your life!

Whatever your profession, choose to be the best. By reading for just ten minutes a day, you can finish a book in a month and join the top 1 percent in the nation in your profession. In addition, place on your nightstand a book of famous quotations, and every morning put a positive thought in your head before you roll out of bed. You could read my collection, *David Cottrell's Collection of Favorite Quotations,* or anyone else's. There are plenty of good ones around. If you start your day with a positive thought, you'll make a positive difference.

Another choice you can make to gain energy through knowledge is to use your commute time wisely. The average person spends more than 500 hours each year commuting—the equivalent of more than twelve forty-hour workweeks! Convert some of that time to energizing yourself and preparing for the workday. The more energized you are during your drive time, the better prepared you will be to face the challenges of your day.

In today's business world, with the explosion of information and technology, continuing education is no longer an option for success—it's a necessity! A PhD earned today is obsolete within five years because information and theories are changing so rapidly. Keep yourself informed, and you'll keep up with changes.

Sharing Knowledge Creates Energy

I'm not sure when or where I heard "the more you learn, the more you earn" the first time, but it was early in my business career. I probably discounted it as someone's attempt to be clever.

Over the years, I've discovered that whoever told me "the more you learn, the more you earn" gave me some of the best advice I've ever received. This revelation led me to discover that the more knowledge you share, the more knowledge you gain.

Several years ago, whenever I hired a new district manager for FedEx, before he or she even met the new team, I paced that person through an intense learning program. For five days, the new manager was asked to read two books a day. Most of the books were brief. The new manager read one book in the morning and one in the afternoon. While reading, he or she identified ten ideas from that particular book to implement when he or she took over the team. Then we discussed each idea before he or she moved on to the next book.

After reading ten books, the new manager had identified one hundred ideas. Some of the concepts were redundant because several of the books covered the same topics. However, the point of this exercise was to mold the manager's concept of leadership during our sessions.

After we developed the list of hundred, the new manager's final task was to narrow the list to ten . . . the top ten leadership priorities.

You may want to try this exercise with your own staff. It will be eye-opening for everyone. The greater payback is that you become energized with their knowledge. These sessions create deep conversation, you get to know your employee better, and you are held accountable for living up to what you are teaching. Knowledge creates energy because you will develop a thirst for learning even more.

And there is a ROI! The more you learn, the more you will earn!

Values Create Energy

Every path in business involves difficult choices that may not be clearly right or wrong, or choices that challenge our faith, commitment, and desire to keep going.

The key to increasing your energy and making the best decisions is to understand your values. What's the one thing that you will not compromise under any circumstance? Until you know your number one value, you cannot commit to numbers two, three, or four.

Your values create your energy to lead. Once you identify

your values, your choices are easier. But compromising your values will instantly drain energy from you and your team.

Values help us be strong in our commitments and consistent in meeting our challenges. The following tips will help.

1. Ensure Your Job Matches Your Values

Many people occupy jobs that are wrong for them, and they're discontented because their professional lives conflict with their values. If you're in that situation, you're guaranteed to be miserable and to make everyone around you miserable too.

You probably know some very intelligent, very successful, but very unhappy people who face a clash of values, day in and day out. Maybe their jobs require constant time away from their families. The money is great, but their families mean much more.

These people will never reach their potential until their values align with their daily lives. You cannot be happy at work if you constantly feel your work is forcing you to compromise your values.

"In order to succeed," Will Rogers said, "you must know what you are doing, like what you are doing, and believe in what you are doing." A passion for your job will create energy and focus for you to lead others. If you're not comfortable telling others what you do, you're likely in the wrong job.

2. Set Personal Goals

You cannot fulfill any dream without first understanding your purpose. It's been said that less than 5 percent of people have personal goals they're actually working to accomplish. Your personal goals are the rudder for your life; they steer you in the right direction. You will not achieve your purpose if you cannot define what you are trying to accomplish.

- Write your personal goals on a sheet of paper. The act of writing things down clarifies what you really want. Write down a detailed description. The more details that you can describe the better.

  Then set a monthly goal and establish what actions are needed to accomplish that goal. Sounds simple, but if you do this for two months, you'll see more satisfaction at work and at home.

- Develop an accountability group. Pick one or two ambitious, fun, positive people whom you admire and meet with them once a week just to talk. This accountability group will help you keep your sanity when you need to talk things out. It's important to have a group to relate to and be yourself with. Pick a group, find the time, choose the place, and lift each other's spirits.

- Mentor others. Everyone needs encouragement from time to time. Make the effort to encourage others, and you'll receive encouragement in return. Several years ago, a survey asked people whether they had a mentor, and 86 percent of respondents said no. Eighty-six percent! People make better decisions when they have a mentor to follow, so it's a good business decision to become a mentor. However, as the mentor, you will receive the greatest return on investment! You will become what you teach, and you will become accountable for your teaching. Mentoring others will pay dividends many times over.

- Keep your sense of humor. When you stop laughing at yourself, you're taking yourself too seriously. Enjoy the different personalities on your team and don't be afraid to admit mistakes or laugh at yourself. Job satisfaction requires a good sense of humor. People who can laugh at life are healthier, happier, and more energized. Use your sense of humor to make life fun!

The tragedy of life is what dies inside a man while he lives.
—ALBERT EINSTEIN

3. Hang In There Long Enough to Win!

Without a doubt, there are some who give up too soon—just before they turn the corner to success. Successful people keep moving even when they are scared and have made mistakes.

The following story illustrates what happens to many on the road to success:

A man meets a guru on the road and asks, "Which way is success?"

The bearded sage doesn't speak, but points to the left.

The man, thrilled by the prospect of quick and easy success, rushes off. Suddenly, there's a loud *SPLAT!*

Eventually, the man limps back, tattered and stunned, assuming he took a wrong turn. So he repeats his question to the guru, who again points silently in the same direction.

The man obediently walks off, and this time there's a deafening *SPLAAAAT!*

When the man crawls back, he is bloody, broken, and irate. "I asked you which way to success!" he screams at the guru. "I followed your direction, but all I got was splatted—twice! No more pointing! Talk!"

Only then does the guru speak, very quietly. "Success is that way. Just a little past splat."

Many of us would be tempted to give up after the first *SPLAT!* But we must develop the courage and resolve to hang in there, through several rounds of splatting, if necessary! If you persevere and work through the issues, you *can* and *will* make a difference.

Great spirits have always encountered violent opposition from mediocre minds.
—ALBERT EINSTEIN

The Leader's Impact on Energy

- Enthusiasm creates energy and produces positive results even when nothing else changes.

- If you want to increase your organization's energy, start by increasing your own energy.

- Complacency is the root of mediocrity.

Monday Morning Discussion Questions

- What lifestyle changes do you need to make in order to increase your physical energy?

- Do you have a plan for your ongoing development and improvement? How do you hold yourself accountable to the plan?

- What are your core values? Are there any areas of your life that are out of sync with those values?

Three Things You Will Do This Week to Increase Your Personal Energy

1. _____
2. _____
3. _____

10

The Final Word

*Anyone who has never made a mistake has never
tried anything new.*
—ALBERT EINSTEIN

The sun emits a billion kilowatts of energy per hour, yet we can deflect most of its harmful effects with an ultrathin application of sunscreen or a visor, which diffuses its energy. On the other hand, a laser beam focuses only a few kilowatts of energy. Yet this relatively weak source of energy can cut a diamond in half or even eradicate certain types of cancer! The role of the leader is to have a laserlike focus on the things that are important for the organization's success.

Albert Einstein's groundbreaking formula $E=mc^2$ was derived when Einstein dared to challenge accepted scientific principles that had not changed since the time of Newton, 200 years before. Einstein's theory radically changed human understanding of the universe and led to significant developments that changed history.

Energy is essential to success in organizations today. If there is no excitement, no enthusiasm, and no passion, there is no catalyst for achievement. Energy is distributed in organizations as motivation—the driving force that people generate to achieve a specific goal. The motivation must be generated daily. Zig Ziglar, one of the greatest motivational speakers of all time, says that "People often say that motivation doesn't last. Well, neither does bathing—that's why we recommend it daily." Everyone needs a daily dose of motivation!

Your organization is an incredible reservoir of energy just waiting to be released. And that is the task of the leader—to find a way to tap into that energy, conduct it, and multiply it throughout the organization.

But in taking on that task, it's important to remember the following:

- *Leaders get what they do.* You are the role model that your team is following. People follow people. More than value statements, mission statements, memos, and e-mails, people follow *you*. You must continually, clearly, and concisely communicate an exciting, authentic, and enthusiastic vision for your people to buy into and treat as their own.

- *The more involved leaders are, the better their decisions.* To lead your people, you must know your people and involve them in your decisions. Most of

the time your team is collectively better informed
than you—all you have to do is ask them the right
questions, and you'll find that they have the right
answers.

• *Get the right people in the right jobs.* Nothing is
more important to the energy of an organization
than having the right people on the team.

Peter Drucker once said that every business failure was the
result of leadership failure. I have found that statement to be
true. Whether it is hiring the wrong people, lack of capital to
sustain the business, chaos within the organization, or just not
paying attention—everything falls at the leader's feet.

When my business was struggling, I attended a seminar
to generate some ideas and energy to reinvest in the business.
The seminar leader asked a simple question: "What two or
three things could happen that would free your business to
succeed?" He made us narrow it down to two or three . . . not
the twenty that we thought would be required. We completed
the task in about five minutes. Everyone thought they knew
where the magic bullets were—more sales, better employees,
more cash, etc.

After reviewing all of the typical answers, the facilitator
then asked the magic question: "Who can be the person to
free your business?" Of course, everyone knew it was us . . .
the owners. There was no real revelation in the answer . . . but
there was a stunned moment when we knew that we had to be
the ones to belly up to the bar and take control and attack the

things holding us and our businesses back. I had looked the answer in the face and the answer was me.

No matter what your organization, title, or experience—you must have the answer to become the most successful person in your field. You are the ultimate energizer. Challenge yourself. Dig deep into the role of a leader. Read all that you can about leadership and become a lifelong learner. Strive to keep your knowledge fresh and your attitude positive. Develop and apply new skills to help accelerate your growth.

Years ago, my father told me that there are two great discoveries that I should search for in business. The first is to discover what I really want to do, and the second is to have the courage, drive, and determination to make it happen.

I pass that same advice on to you.

The average person has great intentions of making a difference. Intentions do not accomplish anything. The people who find success make the conscious decision to step out and make a difference. I hope you will make that decision. It could begin today. It could begin right now.

May life's journey bring you energy, success, and prosperity!

Monday Morning Discussion Questions

- Which of the five energy conductors—synchronization, speed, communication, Customer Passion, and integrity—can have the biggest impact on your team's energy?

- Are you the best role model you can be for your team? In which areas can you improve?

- In what ways can you exponentially affect the energy of your team?

Three Things You Will Do This Week to Energize and Motivate Your Team

1. ⎯⎯⎯⎯⎯⎯⎯⎯⎯⎯⎯⎯⎯⎯⎯⎯⎯⎯⎯⎯⎯⎯⎯⎯⎯⎯
2. ⎯⎯⎯⎯⎯⎯⎯⎯⎯⎯⎯⎯⎯⎯⎯⎯⎯⎯⎯⎯⎯⎯⎯⎯⎯⎯
3. ⎯⎯⎯⎯⎯⎯⎯⎯⎯⎯⎯⎯⎯⎯⎯⎯⎯⎯⎯⎯⎯⎯⎯⎯⎯⎯

Summary

Part One
The Power of Energy and Motivation
The Formula: $E=MC^2$

E = energy

M = your people

C = the conductors of energy:

    Synchronization

    Speed

    Communication

    Customer Passion

    Integrity

^{2} = the leader's impact on the organization

Why Energy and Motivation Leaks Occur

Burnout—constant intense energy over an extended period
of time

Status quo—long periods of consistent performance without
new challenges
Decay—leaks that result from failure to address external or
internal issues

Mass: Building the Right Organization

Team energy is dependent upon the ratio of energizers to
sappers.
A shift in organizational culture occurs when you achieve
critical mass—when enough individuals change their
attitude, thinking, and behavior.
The best leaders are also the best followers.
Organizational energy increases when the forward
momentum of energizers exceeds the negative effects of
the energy sappers.
People support what they help create.
Leadership focus and direction create energy. Leadership
chaos drains organizational energy.

Part Two
The Conductors of Energy and Motivation
Synchronization

Without synchronization, your organization will be
paralyzed, and forward movement will come to a halt.
Synchronization can effectively conduct energy only when
everyone clearly understands what you're trying to
accomplish.
Confusion creates corporate attention deficit disorder.
Clarity and simplicity lead to synchronization and the
accomplishment of objectives.

If it takes you more than thirty seconds to recite your
corporate mission, it is probably too complex.
What gets rewarded gets done.

Speed
To remain on top, successful organizations have to be agile
and react swiftly to changing conditions.
The entire organization is energized by an environment in
which people are appreciated.
Front line employees stay with an organization for one key
reason—because they feel that their supervisors care
about them.
It is vital to take quick, decisive action to stop the energy
leaks caused by underperformers.
Acting quickly to recognize employees can have a tremendous
impact on building loyalty, respect, and trust.
The longer an underperformer remains on the team, the more
energy will be sapped from your team!
Problems do not just go away. Address issues quickly to avoid
larger problems later.

Communication
If there is no trust, it doesn't matter what you communicate.
Don't get so caught up in your leadership position that you're
afraid to ask for honest, candid feedback.
Effective communication is not about you—it's about them!
Knowledge shared is energy multiplied.
Ask the three magic questions: "I don't know . . . what do
you think?" "What business are we in?" and "How is
business?"

The more people learn, the more energized they become at
  work.

Customer Passion

If your customers are unhappy, you will eventually end up
  with unhappy employees too.

Happy customers energize employees.

Dissatisfied customers and dissatisfied employees become ill-
  will ambassadors for your organization.

If you take care of your people, they will take care of your
  customers.

Opportunities to win loyal customers are sometimes cleverly
  disguised as a customer complaint.

Angry customers have elephant-like memories—they never
  forget!

Integrity

One of the toughest things for a leader to figure out is "What
  is the truth?"

If you are a person who searches for the truth—regardless of
  politics or personal agenda—you are a unique and valued
  person.

Integrity is never being ashamed of your reflection.

There can be no positive energy without trust.

The ultimate test of integrity is your follow-through.

Part Three
Optimizing Your Resources
The Leader's Impact on Energy

Enthusiasm creates energy and produces positive results even
  when nothing else changes.

If you want to increase your organization's energy, start by
  increasing your own energy.

Complacency is the root of mediocrity.

Three Ways to Bring *Monday Morning Motivation* into Your Organization

1. Monday Morning Motivation PowerPoint
   Presentation

Introduce and reinforce *Monday Morning Motivation* within your organization with this complete and cost-effective presentation. All the main concepts and ideas in the book are reinforced in this professionally produced, downloadable PowerPoint presentation with facilitator guide and notes. Available at www.CornerStoneLeadership.com for $99.95.

2. Keynote Presentation

Invite author David Cottrell to inspire your team and help create greater success for your organization. Each presentation is designed to set a solid foundation for both organizational and personal success. Contact Michele Lucia at (972) 899-3411 or at Michele@CornerStoneLeadership.com.

3. Monday Morning Motivation Workshop

Facilitated by David Cottrell or a certified CornerStone Leadership instructor, this three-hour or six-hour workshop will reinforce the principles of *Monday Morning Motivation*. Each participant will develop a personal action plan that can make a profound difference in his or her life and career. Visit www. CornerStoneLeadership.com.

Acknowledgments

Without a doubt, I am one of the most fortunate people in the world. I thank God every day for allowing me the opportunity to live my dream.

Special thanks to the following:

My wife for over thirty years, Karen. She has stayed the course with me even when waves were billowing over the top of the seawalls.

My kids—Jennifer, Kimberly, and Michael; my sons-in-law—Kevin and Huntleigh; and my grandson—Noah David. What a privilege to watch them grow!

The CornerStone team—Alice Adams, Juli Baldwin, Barbara Bartlett, Jack Bartlett, Brandon Burwell, Ken Carnes, Lee Colan, Jim Garner, Kathleen Green, Harry Hopkins, Michele Lucia, Suzanne McClelland, Melissa Monogue, and Valerie Sokolowsky. There is no better team.

Thanks to David Hale Smith, my literary agent, and Hollis Heimbouch, of HarperCollins Business, for bringing *Monday Morning Motivation* to life.

My mentors and friends—Ty Deleon, Logan Garrett,

Louis Kruger, Mark Layton, Joe Miles, Tod Taylor, and many others who have stood by me through thick and thin.

Thanks to the 24,000 CornerStone customers who have remained loyal to our work for the past fifteen years.

To each person who reads this book, best wishes in your journey to success!

About the Author

David Cottrell, president and CEO of CornerStone Leadership Institute, is an internationally known leadership consultant, educator, and speaker. His business experience includes leadership positions with Xerox and FedEx. He also led the successful turnaround of a Chapter 11 company before founding CornerStone in 1996.

He is the author of more than twenty-five books, including *Monday Morning Mentoring; Monday Morning Choices; Listen Up, Leader; The Next Level: Leadership Beyond the Status Quo; Monday Morning Leadership; Leadership . . . Biblically Speaking; Management Insights; Leadership Courage; Winners Always Quit,* and *Birdies, Pars, and Bogeys: Leadership Lessons from the Links.*

David is a thought-provoking and electrifying professional speaker. He has presented his leadership message to over 300,000 managers worldwide. His powerful wisdom and insights on leadership have made him a highly sought after keynote speaker and seminar leader. To invite David to speak at your next leadership conference, please contact Michele@CornerStoneLeadership.com.

David and his wife, Karen, reside in Horseshoe Bay, Texas. He can be reached at www.CornerStoneLeadership.com.